COMPANIONS FOR THE JOURNEY

Praying with

Pope John Paul II

Jo Garcia-Cobb and Keith E. Cobb

the WORD
among us®
press

The Word Among Us Press
9639 Doctor Perry Road
Ijamsville, Maryland 21754
www.wordamongus.org

10 09 08 07 06   1 2 3 4 5

ISBN 10: 1-59325-069-X
ISBN 13: 978-1-59325-069-0

Selections from the writings and speeches of Pope John Paul II
reprinted with permission of *Libreria Editrice Vaticana*.

Scripture texts used in this work are taken from the Revised Standard Version
Bible: Catholic Edition, © 1965 and 1966 by the Division of Christian Education of the National Council of the Churches of Christ in the U.S.A. All rights
reserved. Used with permission.

Cover design by The DesignWorks Group
Cover photo: Franco Origlia © Corbis. All Rights Reserved.

Made and printed in the United States of America

Garcia-Cobb, Jo.
Praying with Pope John Paul II / Jo Garcia-Cobb and Keith E. Cobb.
    p. cm.
Includes bibliographical references.
ISBN-13: 978-1-59325-069-0 (alk. paper)
ISBN-10: 1-59325-069-X (alk. paper)
    1. Catholic Church--Prayer-books and devotions--English. I. Cobb, Keith E.,
1947- II. Title.
BX2149.2.G37 2006
242--dc22
                    2006008035

To the elderly, the sick, and the dying
at Providence Benedictine Nursing Center
Mt. Angel, Oregon

⸙

"Prayer is the first expression of man's inner truth,
the first condition for authentic freedom of spirit."
—John Paul II

Acknowledgments

We owe a profound debt of gratitude to the following people whose faith, hope, and love are very much a part of this book:

The Garcia and Cobb families, especially our mothers, Geneva and Remedios, for their prayers and moral support.

Our editors, Patricia Mitchell and Margaret Procario, for their uncompromising faithfulness.

Monsignor Auve Perron, Father Michael Mee, OSB, and Father Christopher LaRocca, OCD, for their spiritual guidance.

John and Gerry Beyer, Don and Sue Sowden, and Marlene Sternhagen and family for the hospitality, encouragement, and generosity they extended to us during the writing of this book.

The ever-supportive librarians at the Mount Angel Abbey Library.

The monks at Mt. Angel Abbey, whose consecrated life of prayer and work for the Lord is a constant source of strength and inspiration.

Our daughter, Anna Maria, our bundle of joy, who kept us going, no matter what.

Contents

Preface

The day of Pope John Paul II's death, April 2, 2005—which also happened to be the vigil of Divine Mercy Sunday—I found myself standing in a long line of people going to confession at the Mount Angel Abbey Church in St. Benedict, Oregon. Deeply saddened by the passing of the only pope I had ever really known and come to love, I turned to the woman on my right and asked how she was feeling about his death. Her answer took me by surprise. With much joy, she exclaimed, "I'm so happy that I don't have to keep wishing to have a private audience with him. Now I can talk with him anytime, anywhere!" "But, yes, of course," I said quietly. I had forgotten that there was actually greater reason to rejoice than to be sorrowful. Following a long and fruitful life, our beloved pope had gone to be with the Lord. And, although we would now be deprived of his physical presence, John Paul II had left us his example to follow, and would be closer to us than ever in prayer.

The former pope's ability to draw people to God was remarkable. Perhaps the most charismatic leader—religious or political—in modern times, as well as an accomplished intellectual, he was at heart a humble man who was able to relate to the struggles and the sufferings of his brothers and sisters. This humility combined with his unwavering faith and his uncompromising ideals had the power to draw even the most unsuspecting unbelievers into God's embrace.

My husband, Keith, and I were among those unsuspecting souls who found themselves moved and astonished by the life and work of this remarkable man. From knowing little or nothing about John Paul II less than a decade ago, we now find ourselves profoundly indebted to him for bringing us back to Christ. I was a lapsed Catholic who had stopped practicing Christianity to explore other religions and spiritual traditions. I had just returned to the Church when I received an unexpected offer in the summer of 1998 to write a pictorial biography of Pope John Paul II. Keith had converted to Catholicism after spending about twenty-five years as a full-time disciple of an East Indian guru. Little did we know that learning and writing about John Paul II's life and work would serve as the key that would open for us spiritual riches we had never before discovered. Through John Paul II's witness to Jesus Christ, we saw the possibility of living a life in true love and freedom—a life whose meaning and purpose surpasses the definitions and tempests of the day.

When trying to describe John Paul II's legacy to the world, it's difficult to resist the temptation to quantify it. Almost every tribute paid to this pope after his death contained the record-breaking figures of his pastoral travels, the volumes he wrote and spoke, the saints he canonized, the dialogues he initiated among divided churches and the world's religions, and the degree to which he helped bring about the fall of Communism in Europe. More telling than the numbers, though, was the universal outpouring of love at his death. Countless people from all walks of life and various religious traditions—from world leaders to peasants in far-flung hamlets—spoke of how John Paul II touched and helped transform their lives. Although the details of their stories differ, these testimonies carry the force of Peter's confession that Christ, indeed, is the Son of the living God (see Matthew 16:15-16). Although made some two thousand years ago, Peter's confession of faith came alive in countless hearts as people saw in John Paul II a shepherd whose life was completely given over to Christ and his flock. This successor to Peter tended, fed, and strengthened Christ's flock to the very end, as he taught us how to live and how to die for God's glory (see John 21:15-19). Through God's work in the life of John Paul II, people like ourselves were led not only to a conviction that Jesus is Lord of our life and of all creation, but to a profound encounter with him as the Son of the living God.

John Paul II imparted to us the legacy of his own incredible faith. Rooted in prayer, this legacy can take root in our own prayer life. In this book, we explore this lasting legacy and prayerfully ponder the ways that it can continue to grow and bear fruit in our lives and in the lives of those around us.

Our prayer for you as you read this book echoes John Paul II's prayer for the Church to contemplate the face of Christ as intimately as his mother, Mary, did. Such contemplation is at the heart of the program for evangelization that John Paul II set before the Church at the dawn of the new millennium. May you recognize the Lord wherever he manifests himself, but above all, in his living presence in the Eucharist.

Jo Garcia-Cobb and Keith E. Cobb

Introduction

Man achieves the fullness of prayer not
when he expresses himself,
but when he lets God be most fully present in prayer.
—John Paul II, *Crossing the Threshold of Hope*

This book is meant to assist your journey into a deeper prayer life with the example and guidance of a fellow pilgrim, Pope John Paul II. In drawing from his life and work, from his youth through the twenty-sixth year of his papacy, it offers much food for prayer, inspiration, and practical guidance to people from all walks of life. It is both a celebration and a contemplation of God's work in the life of John Paul II. As our lives intersect his, we are infused with the light of Christ.

Anyone familiar with the life of John Paul II knows that his many accomplishments were the fruit of intense prayer. Fr. Christopher LaRocca, OCD, a Carmelite priest who has lectured on John Paul II's spirituality and had the experience of praying with him in the same chapel, gives us this insight into the pope's approach to prayer:

> With his understanding of the mystical body of Christ, he was able to embrace the whole Church, the whole world in prayer. As priest and as vicar of Christ, the Mass was the center of his life. In mystically entering the paschal mystery, he carried the weight of the whole Church

on his shoulders. As he entered into the dark night, he also received the light of the resurrection. He prayed as if he was being crushed like a grape. He would groan during the prayers before and after Mass. This is not a negative thing. It's a blessing to enter into the passion and resurrection of the Lord. From being united with the Lord in this way, he emerged as a prophet.[1]

Praying with the help of this book is a lot like praying with John Paul II in the same chapel. As Fr. LaRocca's experience suggests, the intensity of the pope's prayer life has a way of inspiring us to ponder the intimacy with which John Paul II approached the Lord in prayer.

JOHN PAUL II ON HOW BEST TO PRAY

When he was asked how one can best engage in prayer and dialogue with Christ, John Paul II suggested starting with Saint Paul's Letter to the Romans: "The apostle comes to the heart of the matter when he writes: 'The Spirit too comes to the aid of our weakness; for we do not know how to pray as we ought, but the Spirit himself intercedes with inexpressible groanings' (Romans 8:26)."[2]

Our weakness, John Paul II goes on to explain, comes in believing that our prayer originates with us. Prayer, he observes, "is commonly held to be a conversation. In a conversation, there are always an 'I' and a 'thou' or 'you.' In this case, the 'Thou' is with a capital T. If at first the 'I' seems to be the most important element in prayer, prayer teaches that the situation is actually different. The 'Thou' is more important, because our prayer begins with God."[3]

So, contrary to how it may seem to us, the one who takes the lead role in prayer is God. John Paul II: "In prayer, then, the true protagonist is God. The protagonist is Christ. . . . The protagonist is the Holy Spirit, who 'comes to the aid of our weakness.' We begin to pray, believing that it is our own initiative that compels us to do so. Instead, we learn that it is always God's initiative within us, just as Saint Paul has written."[4] As John Paul II teaches us, "Man achieves the fullness of prayer not when he expresses himself, but when he lets God be most fully present in prayer."[5]

ON USING THIS BOOK FOR LECTIO DIVINA (DIVINE READING)

One way of opening ourselves to God's presence in prayer is through sacred reading, or *lectio divina,* which is recommended by John Paul II as an essential element of spiritual formation. In his apostolic exhortation *Ecclesia in America* (On the Encounter with the Living Jesus Christ), the pope advises that "the Church in America 'must give a clear priority to prayerful reflection on Sacred Scripture by all the faithful.' This reading of the Bible, accompanied by prayer, is known in the tradition of the Church as *lectio divina,* and it is a practice to be encouraged among all Christians."[6]

Although *lectio divina* is recommended specifically for Scripture, it may be used with any substantial spiritual work, as long as it is done with the intention to know and encounter Jesus Christ in the process. Readers would do well to approach this book in *lectio divina*—that is, not so much to gather information, but to let the word of God in Scripture, and as lived by John Paul II, permeate our soul.

The practice of *lectio divina* involves four steps: *lectio, meditatio, oratio,* and *contemplatio.*

Lectio is reverential reading. In *lectio*, we read slowly and attentively, gently listening to hear a word or phrase that is God's word for us.

Meditatio is pondering a word or a passage that speaks to us in a personal way. The image of the ruminant animal quietly chewing its cud was used in antiquity as a symbol of the Christian pondering the word of God. Christians have always seen a scriptural invitation to *lectio divina* in the example of the Virgin Mary "pondering in her heart" what she saw and heard about her son (Luke 2:19). Through *meditatio*, we allow God's word to touch us and transform us.

Oratio is prayer understood both as dialogue with God—that is, as loving conversation—and as consecration. Just as a priest consecrates the elements of bread and wine at the eucharistic celebration, God invites us in *lectio divina* to offer ourselves up to him, as we allow our lives to be filled with the light of his word.

Contemplatio is resting in God's presence, as we let go of our own thoughts and concerns. No one who has ever been in love needs to be reminded that there are moments in loving relationships when words are unnecessary. It is the same in our relationship with God. In contemplation, we simply let God's loving presence embrace us in the silence of our hearts.

PRAYING WITH JOHN PAUL II

Praying with Pope John Paul II consists of fifteen meditations based on some of the most important themes in the life of John Paul II. Each of these themes imparts a gospel message, as John Paul II lived and taught it in the context of a pivotal time in his life and in the life of the Church and the world. Concurrently, these themes shed light on some of the most fundamental, yet oftentimes perplexing, challenges in our pursuit of God's will in our own lives.

The meditations in this book can best be approached when we can be still and silent before God and are open to the promptings of the Holy Spirit.

Following are brief descriptions of how each theme unfolds and what each meditation offers:

The Fruit of Prayer Is Mission helps us to see where our prayer life stands before God and offers guidance to help it progress into union with God.

Be Not Afraid inspires us to follow God's call to participate in his work and to let go of the fears that keep us from saying yes to him.

The Spirit Gives Life shows how the Holy Spirit can radically transform our life and the life of the world when we allow him to do his work in and through us.

The Church of the Eucharist helps us to more fully recognize and receive Jesus Christ in the Blessed Sacrament, the Church's greatest treasure.

Mary, Our Mother, helps us to be faithful to Jesus' command, "Behold your Mother" (John 19:27), as we let the Blessed Mother lead us on the path of perfect discipleship.

The Gospel of Life leads us to raise a great prayer for life and to build a culture of life through prayer, fasting, service, and activism.

Aging in Grace inspires us to approach our twilight years with joy, thanksgiving, and a more intensified prayer life, as well as to follow John Paul II's example to serve God to our last breath.

Youth: Future of the Church and the World helps us to journey with our youth in discovering the highest truth and the greatest happiness in following Jesus Christ.

The Gift of Marriage and Sexuality helps us to live married, religious, and single lives in sacramental grace and to realize the deepest meaning and purpose of human sexuality.

The Domestic Church focuses on our family as our first mission field, and guides us in making our home a school of prayer and training in the faith.

Penance, Forgiveness, and Reconciliation helps us to see what it takes to be truly reconciled with God and neighbor, as we learn from John Paul II's example of a truly penitential life.

The Christian Meaning of Suffering takes us into the meaning and value of suffering when seen in the light of Christ's passion, death, and resurrection. It inspires us to draw strength in prayer and in the sacraments in times of suffering.

That We May All Be One inspires us to pray Jesus' prayer for unity for all Christians and for all humanity in light of John Paul II's efforts to promote ecumenical prayer and interreligious prayer for world peace.

Truth and Freedom helps us to anchor our lives in truth and to stand up for truth amid the moral confusion that besets our world.

The **Springtime of Evangelization** empowers us with John Paul II's vision of the new evangelization, as it strengthens us to fulfill Christ's commission to be fishers of men.

How to Use the Meditations

The format of each meditation is designed to help us contemplate God's work in the life of John Paul II so that it can take deep root and bear abundant fruit in our own lives. Each meditation unfolds in the following manner:

Theme: Each meditation opens with a theme that distills a gospel message, as it was lived out and preached by John Paul II. Spend some time reflecting on this theme as you open your heart to receive the grace to enter into God's presence in meditation.

Opening Prayer: We praise and thank God for the grace he has bestowed upon us to live out the particular gospel message contained in the meditation. Spend some time pondering this grace in your heart before moving on.

About John Paul II: This is a slice from the life of John Paul II that shows us how he sought to do God's will during some of the most momentous, as well as some of the most trying, times of his life—and how God led him through these times. Take a moment to reflect upon how John Paul II's experience speaks to your own life. A point of reflection is suggested in the *Pause* question.

John Paul II's Words: These excerpts from John Paul II's writings and spoken messages offer much wisdom, depth, and inspiration. Make sure to highlight passages that you find particularly helpful or that speak to you in a special way. "Chew on" these passages, as in *lectio divina*.

Reflection: This section allows us to reflect upon John Paul II's experience and his message as they address some of the most significant challenges we face in living our lives as Christians in today's world. Included in this section:

Questions for personal reflection and faith sharing help us to focus on areas of our lives that can be deepened and enriched by John Paul II's example and guidance. Several questions are offered to address the needs of readers in various phases of their Christian journey. It would be best, at any given time, to focus on one question that strikes you most deeply and offers the most meaningful opportunity for reflection or faith sharing. This is also a good opportunity to record your reflections in a journal so that you can enter into a deeper dialogue with God. One recommended method of journaling is to write prayerful letters to God.

Guidance for prayer and action offers a variety of suggestions for prayer, study, and charitable work to help us live out both the vertical and horizontal dimensions of the cross—our ascent to God in prayer and communion with neighbor.

God's Word: These are Scripture passages that convey the essence of the given meditation. Consider this food for *lectio divina.*

Closing Prayer: This prayer is, in most cases, from John Paul II himself. Feel free to make it your own and to add your own intentions.

USES FOR THIS BOOK

Praying with Pope John Paul II may be used for **personal prayer,** for **individual retreat,** for **group prayer and faith sharing,** or for **group retreat.** While the section above offers sufficient guidance to those who wish to use this book for personal prayer, those using this book for group prayer may find the following points helpful.

SUGGESTIONS FOR USE WITH A GROUP

Choose a facilitator for the group to help keep the discussion focused and to ensure that each participant has an opportunity to contribute. The same person could serve as facilitator for every session, or participants could take turns facilitating different sessions.

Ask participants to read the meditation before the meeting and to consider which of the questions for reflection and faith sharing, and which of the suggestions for prayer and action, seem most relevant to them. Preparing ahead will allow more time for faith sharing and lead to more fruitful discussions.

Remind participants of the time limitations of the meeting in order to give everyone a chance to speak and to accomplish the goals for the session. At the discretion of the group, you may decide to spend additional time on a particular question or activity, or to continue the discussion at another time.

Try to engage in at least one prayerful activity during each meeting. Participants may choose from the activities suggested but should also be encouraged to come up with other ideas. Members are encouraged to carry out additional activities beyond the meeting.

"Go Forth and Bear Fruit"

"You did not choose me, but I chose you and appointed you that you should go and bear fruit" (John 15:16). In his apostolic exhortation on the vocation and mission of the laity, John Paul II writes that "bearing fruit is an essential demand of life in Christ and life in the Church." He adds that "communion with Jesus, which gives rise to the communion of Christians among themselves, is an indispensable condition for bearing fruit."[7] May the meditations in this book be an opportunity for you to enter into a deeper communion with Jesus Christ, and to bear abundant and lasting fruit in his vineyard.

1. Christopher LaRocca, interview by Jo Garcia-Cobb, Mt. Angel, Oregon, January 1, 2006.
2. John Paul II, *Crossing the Threshold of Hope,* ed. Vittorio Messori (New York: Alfred A. Knopf, Inc., 1994), p. 16.
3. John Paul II, *Crossing the Threshold of Hope,* p. 16.
4. John Paul II, *Crossing the Threshold of Hope,* p. 17.
5. John Paul II, *Crossing the Threshold of Hope,* p. 18.
6. John Paul II, Apostolic Exhortation *Ecclesia in America* (On the Encounter with the Living Jesus Christ: The Way to Conversion, Communion and Solidarity in America), January 22, 1999, 31.
7. John Paul II, Apostolic Exhortation *Christifideles Laici* (On the Vocation and the Mission of the Lay Faithful in the Church and in the World), December 30, 1988, 32.

The Fruit of Prayer Is Mission

Theme: We need to "put out into the deep" (Luke 5:4) of prayer in order to fulfill our mission.

Opening prayer: "O Lord, may my soul be flooded with your light and know you more and more profoundly! Lord, give me so much love. Love forever, serene and generous, that I will be united with you always! Lord, let me serve you, and serve you well on the pathways that you wish to open to my existence here below."[1]

ABOUT JOHN PAUL II

Karol Wojtyla began his journey into the depths of prayer when he met a man who opened the door to a "world I did not yet know." It was in 1940, the second year of the Nazi occupation in Poland, that the twenty-year-old Wojtyla encountered Jan Tyranowski, a tailor by trade and, as Karol wrote in his tribute to his spiritual mentor, an "apostle" by vocation.

Tyranowski was one of the laymen asked by the Salesian fathers to carry on their youth programs at St. Stanislaw Parish in Debniki. Many Salesians, members of a community founded by St. John Bosco, had been rounded up by the Gestapo and shipped to concentration camps. Eleven of the priests in Karol's parish, including the pastor, died in these camps. Along with some fifty young men, Karol received his catechism from Tyranowski in a clandestine ministry that put the lives of both the catechists and the youth at great risk. At the time, the Gestapo was aggressively cracking down on youth groups, many of which had become hotbeds of resistance.

The depth of Tyranowski's spiritual life "showed God" to the young Karol "much more immediately than any sermon or book" could have. "He proved to us that one could not only inquire about God, but that one could live with God," Karol wrote in his first published essay, *Apostol*. One could not spend hours with Jan, he recalled, without concluding that sanctity was everyone's vocation in the Church. In witnessing Tyranowski's profoundly integrated life of prayer and mission, Wojtyla "saw the beauty of the soul opened up by grace," and was drawn to prayer not only as a means of entering God's presence, but as a way of dwelling in God and participating in God's own life.

Tyranowski introduced Karol to the writings of his own teachers in prayer, Saints John of the Cross and Teresa of Avila. Karol's interest in the life and work of these mystics and doctors of the Church grew over the years and planted in him the desire to become a Carmelite monk. Although he eventually took a different path, the contemplative inclination that surfaced in him during Tyranowski's mentorship continued to bear lasting fruit, not only for Karol but for the Church as well. Throughout his priestly life and his papacy, he was able to convey, from a profound level of experience and conviction, that the mystical experience of union with God is not just for cloistered monks and nuns, but is the center of *every* Christian life. Far from being an abstract ideal, union with Christ is a concrete gift that the Holy Spirit instills in us. We, in turn, can accept this gift and respond to it, through contemplation of the divine mysteries and through personal and social action.

Pause: What is my response to John Paul II's teaching that the mystical experience of union with God is for every Christian? How does this challenge me to deepen my prayer life?

JOHN PAUL II'S WORDS

The great mystical tradition of the Church of both East and West . . . shows how prayer can progress as a genuine dialogue of love, to the point of rendering the person wholly possessed by the divine Beloved, vibrating at the Spirit's touch, resting filially within the Father's heart. This is the lived experience of Christ's promise: "He who loves me will be loved by my Father, and I will love him and manifest myself to him (John 14:21)." It is a journey totally sustained by grace, which nonetheless demands an intense spiritual commitment and is no stranger to painful purifications (the "dark night"). But it leads, in various possible ways, to the ineffable joy experienced by the mystics as "nuptial union." How can we forget here, among the many shining examples, the teachings of St. John of the Cross and St. Teresa of Avila?

Yes, dear brothers and sisters, our Christian communities must become genuine "schools" of prayer, where the meeting with Christ is expressed not just in imploring help but also in thanksgiving, praise, adoration, contemplation, listening, and ardent devotion, until the heart truly "falls in love." Intense prayer, yes, but it does not distract us from our commitment to history: by opening our heart to the love of God it also opens it to the love of our brothers and sisters, and makes us capable of shaping history according to God's plan.[2]

Reflection

It took a man of deep prayer and communion with God to help the young Karol Wojtyla venture into the depths of mystical prayer. There was nothing extraordinary about Tyranowski by way of charisma, eloquence, or intellectual prowess that made Karol want to participate in his clandestine classes. In fact, as Karol recalled, Tyranowski had nothing original to say, as he mostly quoted the catechism verbatim. But his interior life, a hidden life whose light spoke to Karol's heart, said plenty, drawing Karol into the mission that God had prepared for him.

Prayer, as the masters of Carmelite spirituality taught it and as John Paul II practiced it, is a heart-to-heart conversation between friends—intimacy with Christ. It is experiencing God's presence as closer to us than our own breath. It is knowing that he listens to every word we utter in prayer. To "contemplate" means to ponder the Word of God, Jesus himself, as Mary did, and to bring the Word to the world. As a mystic and a prophet, John Paul II entered into the paschal mystery through his own personal prayer and emerged to proclaim the Word.

Many of those who witnessed John Paul II in prayer and at work knew that his prayer life was at the core of his immensely fruitful vocation. He showed us that the great catch begins when we cast ourselves into the depths of prayer, where our lives can be wholly conformed to God's will and serve as God's own net for drawing others into his kingdom.

Questions for personal reflection and faith sharing:

Is my heart a genuine school of prayer, open to the promptings and guidance of the Holy Spirit? Is my home a school of prayer? Is my parish committed to helping deepen the prayer life of all its members? What contribution can I make to help deepen the prayer life of members in my community?

Which areas of my prayer life, such as thanksgiving, praise, adoration, contemplation, listening, or ardent devotion, need strengthening? What steps can I take to strengthen them?

How might the study of Christian contemplative prayer help deepen my prayer life? To those who have benefited from the practice of contemplative prayer: share with others what this practice has meant in your life.

❧ How may the Holy Spirit be inviting me to mystical prayer? What habits or situations hinder me from developing a deeper interior life? What can I do to more fully allow the Holy Spirit to lead me in prayer?

Guidance for prayer and action:

❧ Ask the Lord to show you the state of your prayer life. Ask, "Is my prayer life bearing the fruits of ever-deepening love for God and neighbor, of radical self-giving, and of a joy and a peace that nothing can take away from me? Does my heart burn in recognizing Jesus at the eucharistic table? Do I fear offending the Lord and repent of my sins? Am I becoming increasingly open and responsive to the promptings of the Holy Spirit?"

❧ John Paul II emphasizes the vital need for silence in one's search for intimacy with God.[3] Regularly carve out some time to be silent before God each day by turning off your TV, radio, and phone. Savor the silence as you lift your heart to the Lord. Meditate on Psalm 46:10: "Be still, and know that I am God." During a time of quiet prayer, preferably with your eyes closed to draw your attention within, open your heart to God's presence. Let your breathing slow down until you begin to experience a deep stillness. Pray, "Speak, Lord, if you will. I am listening." Then spend as much time as you can listening to God or just being with him in the silence of your heart.

❧ Mine the depths and riches of the Church's prayer life. Start by reading the section on prayer (Part IV) in the *Catechism of the Catholic Church*. If you wish to explore various practices of meditation and contemplative prayer, read the *Letter to the Bishops of the Catholic Church on Some Aspects of Christian Meditation*, issued by the Congregation for the Doctrine of the Faith during John Paul II's pontificate. This letter addresses the need for sure criteria for the practice of different forms of meditation that are faithful to the truth revealed in Jesus Christ.

❧ Let the Holy Spirit guide you in composing a discipline of prayer and meditation that fits with the demands of your vocation. If you're a busy parent, for instance, discuss with your family and friends how you can find quiet time with God. Perhaps they can offer you support such as babysitting. Integrate work and leisure time with prayer time. Sing a prayer or listen to sacred music while doing household chores. How about waking half and hour earlier than usual to read Scripture?

❧ Make it a point to be fully present to and to recognize Christ in every person you encounter. John Paul II was known for his ability to maintain this "contemplative gaze." He was fully present to each person he met, even if the encounter lasted only for a few seconds.

❧ When reading the lives of the saints, pay special attention to the fusion of their interior life and their work in the world and how each sustained the other. John Paul II's apostolic letter

Master in the Faith, written to commemorate the fourth centenary of the death of St. John of the Cross, provides a good exposition of how that saint's inner life translated into lasting fruit in the world.[4]

☙ Join or start a group that meets regularly for prayer and Scripture study.

God's Word

While the people pressed upon him to hear the word of God, [Jesus] was standing by the lake of Gennesaret. And he saw two boats by the lake; but the fishermen had gone out of them and were washing their nets. Getting into one of the boats, which was Simon's, he asked him to put out a little from the land. And he sat down and taught the people from the boat. And when he had ceased speaking, he said to Simon, "Put out into the deep and let down your nets for a catch."

—Luke 5:1-4

Closing prayer: Lord, help us to always take you at your word in prayer and in the mission you have set before us and your Church. May the fruits of our prayer and our labor speak only of you. May we make your love known to everyone we serve and encounter. Amen.

1. John Paul II, *The Private Prayers of John Paul II,* trans. Ann Goldstein (New York: Pocket Books, 1994), p. 197.
2. John Paul II, Apostolic Letter *Novo Millennio Ineunte* (At the Beginning of the New Millennium), January 6, 2001, 33.
3. John Paul II, Homily, Pontifical Athenaeum in Pune, February 10, 1986, 3.
4. John Paul II, Apostolic Letter *Master in the Faith,* December 14, 1990.

MEDITATION TWO

Be Not Afraid

Theme: Do not be afraid to say yes to God.

Opening prayer: Thank you, Father, for calling us to participate in your own life. Grant us the grace to never be afraid to put our lives faithfully and confidently in your hands, and to commit our lives to the fulfillment of your marvelous work.

ABOUT JOHN PAUL II

On September 29, 1978, Cardinal Wojtyla had just finished morning Mass when a staff member quietly informed him that Pope John Paul I had died the previous night—only thirty-four days after having been elected pope. Wojtyla froze. For a long moment, a dead silence fell upon the room. "No," Wojtyla murmured. Quietly, he excused himself and went to his chapel where he shut himself up for several hours.[1]

Wojtyla had reason to pray. He had a strong presentiment of what was to come in two weeks when a new conclave would convene to elect the next pope. Wojtyla was well known and well liked, and had received votes at the last conclave. There was deep division over the two leading Italian cardinals, making it doubtful that either one could win a two-thirds-majority vote. And a growing sentiment had arisen among the cardinals that the next pope would have to be younger, more vigorous, and quite possibly a non-Italian.

In the days that followed, what had begun for Wojtyla as a strong presentiment turned into an ever greater certainty. As it did, Wojtyla became more and more anxious. On the morning of the third day of the conclave, it became clear that there was a deadlock between the two leading Italian candidates. In an atmosphere of growing concern, the cardinals began looking elsewhere for a suitable candidate. By the second ballot of the day, support for Wojtyla had surged dramatically. That afternoon, Wojtyla visited Cardinal Wyszynski, the primate of Poland, and collapsed in his arms, agitated and weeping. Throughout the afternoon, in an atmosphere of tense silence, the cardinals, in groups and individually, prayed and voted, prayed and voted again.

At approximately 5:15 p.m., the fourth and final ballot of the day was tallied. Halfway through the tally, Wojtyla dropped his head into his hands, weighed down by the enormity of what was taking place. Then the result was announced: ninety-nine out of 108 cardinals had given Wojtyla their vote. Cardinal Villot, president of the college of cardinals, made his way over to the desk where Wojtyla sat. "*Acceptasne electionem?*" he asked. Wojtyla looked up, the tension suddenly gone from his face, and with firmness and resolution responded, "In the obedience of faith before Christ my Lord, abandoning myself to the Mother of Christ and the Church, and conscious of the great difficulties, *accepto.*"

Pause: What was at the root of Karol Wojtyla's unconditional yes to God?

JOHN PAUL II'S WORDS

It is one of the great paradoxes of our time that man, who began the period we call "modernity" with a self-confident assertion of his "coming of age" and "autonomy," approaches the end of the twentieth century fearful of himself, fearful of what he might be capable of, fearful for the future. . . .

In order to ensure that the new millennium now approaching will witness a new flourishing of the human spirit, mediated through an authentic culture of freedom, men and women must learn to conquer fear. We must learn not to be afraid, we must rediscover a spirit of hope and a spirit of trust. Hope is not empty optimism springing from a naive confidence that the future will necessarily be better than the past. Hope and trust are the premise of responsible activity and are nurtured in that inner sanctuary of conscience where "man is alone with God" and he thus perceives that he is not alone amid the enigmas of existence, for he is surrounded by the love of the Creator![2]

Do not be afraid! Open wide the doors for Christ! Do not be afraid, I say, because great courage is required if we are to open the doors to Christ, if we are to let Christ enter into our hearts so fully that we can say with St. Paul, "The life I live now is not my own; Christ is living in me" (Galatians 2:20). . . . You need courage to follow Christ, especially when you recognize that so much of our dominant culture is a culture of flight from God. . . . You must not be afraid to confront the "wisdom of this world" with the certainty of the teachings of Christ in which you are grounded, but above all with the love of Christ, with the compassion and the mercy of Christ who, like the Father, desires everyone to be saved and to come to the knowledge of the truth (1 Timothy 2:4). . . .Open the doors of your hearts in order that Christ may enter and bring you his joy.[3]

REFLECTION

How extraordinarily daunting and complex it must have been to lead the Roman Catholic Church, especially at this time in history. Yet, in accepting that responsibility, Pope John Paul II set an example of the faith and hope that would be one of the main themes of his papacy. It is a theme that has characterized Christianity ever since Peter stepped out of the cenacle on Pentecost to proclaim the gospel. How fortunate we are that others through the ages, overcoming their fears, have said yes when called to a vocation within the body of Christ. How fortunate we are that Mary said yes; that the apostles said yes; that our priests, bishops, monks, nuns, fathers, and mothers said yes; and that all the popes, past and present, said yes.

Questions for personal reflection and faith sharing:

❧ Is there something that God is calling me to do that I am afraid to consider?

❧ What are the fears that bind me and keep me from following God's will for my life? How can I confront these fears?

❧ Is there anything that is keeping me from being anchored in the certainty of Christ's love and his teachings? How is God calling me to overcome my uncertainty?

Guidance for prayer and action:

❧ Hold fast to Christ's presence in the Eucharist. Frequent reception of the Holy Eucharist and participating in eucharistic adoration gives us the grace to set our sights on the Lord so that we won't sink before the task God has set before us. John Paul II attributed the inner strength he experienced, especially amid seemingly insurmountable challenges, to eucharistic adoration and daily reception of the Eucharist.

❧ As a guided meditation, individually or in a group, read the canticle of the three faith-filled Hebrew youths who were condemned by King Nebuchadnezzar of Babylon to burn to death in a flaming furnace (Daniel 3:19-24). Imagine the fear they must have experienced as they were being led to the furnace, and the intensity with which they must have prayed. Feel the joyfulness of their praise for the Lord when, as they were being thrown into the furnace, the angel appeared and made them feel as though a dew-laden breeze were blowing through the furnace, surrounding and protecting them. In meditating upon this canticle, John Paul II said that "the force of prayer that is pure, intense, and total in its abandonment to God can dissolve all fears and nightmares."[4]

❧ Receive strength from God's words by praying repeatedly, "I am with you" (Jeremiah 1:8). John Paul II reminds us that human weakness is not an obstacle when we know how to recognize it and place it faithfully and confidently in the hands of God.[5]

❧ Offer your vocation to God during the offertory of the Mass, along with the fears that you encounter in fulfilling it. "In offering yourself to God, pray that your vocation may be spiritually fruitful for the Church, for others, for all to whom we are sent and, in the end, for ourselves. First for others, then for ourselves, because, like Christ, our calling is to serve."[6]

❧ Write in a prayer journal about occasions in your life when God delivered you from weakness of spirit, mind, or body as you had to accomplish a difficult task. Let these experiences remind you of God's unfailing love. Be willing to strengthen others by sharing these stories with them. John Paul II reminds us that God's ways are not our ways—that "inner strength does not follow physical laws" when we rely on the Lord.[7]

Read and share stories of men and women of the Church who conquered their fears as they said yes to God. John Paul II exhorts us to look to Mary as our model in living a life of complete surrender to God. Among many other wonderful models of surrender are Saints Benedict, Catherine of Sienna, and Joan of Arc.

&. Through song, poetry, or in some other creative way, praise and thank God for the grace to participate in his work through whatever calling he has given you in life. Make this a part of your spiritual legacy to your loved ones.

GOD'S WORD

In the fourth watch of the night he came to them, walking on the sea. But when the disciples saw him walking on the sea, they were terrified, saying, "It is a ghost!" And they cried out for fear. But immediately he spoke to them, saying, "Take heart, it is I; have no fear."

And Peter answered him, "Lord, if it is you, bid me come to you on the water." He said, "Come." So Peter got out of the boat and walked on the water and came to Jesus; but when he saw the wind, he was afraid, and beginning to sink he cried out, "Lord, save me." Jesus immediately reached out his hand and caught him, saying to him, "O man of little faith, why did you doubt?" And when they got into the boat, the wind ceased. And those in the boat worshipped him, saying, "Truly you are the Son of God."

—Matthew 14:25-33

Closing prayer: Dear Lord, thank you for saving us from sinking before the tasks you have set before us. Help us to always fix our gaze on you, and to always remember that our lives rest in your hands. Amen.

1. George Weigel, *Witness to Hope* (New York: HarperCollins, 2001), p. 248.
2. John Paul II, Address to the United Nations General Assembly, October 5, 1995, 16.
3. John Paul II, Address at Vespers at Saint Joseph's Seminary, New York, October 6, 1995, 4.
4. John Paul II, General Audience, July 10, 2002, 2.
5. John Paul II, Homily on Fidelity to the Priestly Vocation, Olaya Herrera Airport of Medellin, July 5, 1986, 3.
6. John Paul II, Address to Seminarians, Pontifical Major Seminary of Rome, October 22, 1987.
7. John Paul II, Homily, Celebration for John Paul II's 50th Jubilee of Priestly Ordination, November 7, 1996, 5.

The Spirit Gives Life

Theme: The Holy Spirit can radically change people and events.

Opening prayer: "Come, Holy Spirit, send us from heaven a ray of your light. Come, father of the poor. Come, giver of gifts. Come, light of hearts. Come, sweet guest of the soul, most sweet relief. In toil, give us rest. In heat, give us shelter. In tears, give us comfort. Wash what is unclean. Water what is parched. Heal what bleeds. Bend what is rigid. Warm what is cold. Straighten what is crooked."[1]

ABOUT JOHN PAUL II

On the evening of May 30, 1979, John Paul II spoke to thousands of pilgrims at his weekly audience: "In a few days, on the jubilee of St. Stanislaus, I will have the fortune to go to Poland, to my native land. I shall celebrate Pentecost, the feast of the descent of the Holy Spirit." Alluding to his hopes for peace and religious freedom in Poland and all of Communist-dominated central and eastern Europe, he continued, "I wish to serve this important cause of our times in order that the great works of God may continue to be proclaimed with faith and courage as the seed of hope and love which Christ grafted in us, by means of the Gift of Pentecost. . . . I will pray to the Lord, and I am sure that you will pray with me, that each one will carry out this duty with a sense of responsibility and maturity, inspired by the deep dictates of his own conscience."[2]

In Poland a few days later, under the watchful eyes of Communist authorities, John Paul II drew millions to his public addresses, consolidating an unprecedented measure of hope and strength among the people. As he ended his first Mass in Warsaw's Victory Square, he offered a prayer: "I cry on the vigil of Pentecost, let your Spirit descend. Let your Spirit descend, and renew the face of the earth, the face of this land. Amen."[3]

When John Paul II's plane landed at Okecie Airport, church bells rang throughout the country. He crisscrossed his beloved Poland, deluged by adoring crowds. In nine days he preached thirty-two sermons. Author Bogdan Szajkowski described the pope's visit as "a psychological earthquake, an opportunity for mass political catharsis."[4] The Poles who turned out by the millions looked around and saw that they were not alone. In fact, they were a powerful multitude. The pope spoke of human dignity, the right to religious freedom, and a revolution of the spirit—not insurrection. The people listened. As biographer George Weigel observed, "It was a lesson in dignity, a national plebiscite, Poland's second baptism."[5]

In 1980, shortly after John Paul II's visit, the Solidarity Movement was born in Gdansk. As it grew, it began to inspire anti-Communist movements across eastern and central Europe. The seeds of hope and change that John Paul II planted during that nine-day visit to Poland set in motion a nonviolent revolution that swept Communist Europe, eventually dismantling the reign of Communism, bringing down the Iron Curtain, and ending the Cold War.

Millions of people spread the revolution, but it began with the pope's trip home in 1979. As General Wojciech Jaruzelski said, "That was the detonator."[6] Referring to the pope, Solidarity leader Lech Walesa observed, "Without him there would be no end of Communism or, at least, it would have come much later and the end would have been bloody."[7] After the demise of the Soviet Union, ex-president Mikhail Gorbachev wrote in 1992, "Everything that happened in eastern Europe during these past few years would have been impossible without the pope."[8] During an interview with the writer and producer of a PBS special on John Paul II, Jaruzelski himself remarked that "the Holy Spirit works in mysterious ways."[9]

Pause: What strikes me the most about the way the Cold War came to an end in Europe and the part that John Paul II played in it?

JOHN PAUL II'S WORDS

Whenever the Spirit intervenes, he leaves people astonished. He brings about events of amazing newness; he radically changes persons and history.[10]

The Holy Spirit, in his mysterious bond of divine communion with the Redeemer of man, is the one who brings about the continuity of his work: he takes from Christ and transmits to all, unceasingly entering into the history of the world through the heart of man. Here he becomes—as the liturgical Sequence of the Solemnity of Pentecost proclaims—the true "father of the poor, giver of gifts, light of hearts"; he becomes the "sweet guest of the soul," whom the Church unceasingly greets on the threshold of the inmost sanctuary of every human being. For he brings "rest and relief" in the midst of toil, in the midst of the work of human hands and minds; he brings "rest" and "ease" in the midst of the heat of the day, in the midst of the anxieties, struggles, and perils of every age; he brings "consolation," when the human heart grieves and is tempted to despair. . . . The Church with her heart which embraces all human hearts implores from the Holy Spirit that happiness which only in God has its complete realization: the joy "that no one will be able to take away," (John 16:22) the joy which is the fruit of love, and therefore of God who is love; she implores "the righteousness, the peace, and the joy of the Holy Spirit" in which, in the words of St. Paul, consists the Kingdom of God (Romans 14:17; Galatians 5:22).[11]

REFLECTION

The world had lived under the shadow of the Cold War for forty-six years before it formally came to an end on December 31, 1991, with the dissolution of the Soviet Union. By then, Karol Wojtyla had spent most of his life in Nazi-occupied and then Communist-occupied Poland. Some of his dear friends, both Jews and Christians, were victims of the Holocaust, and he himself worked under forced labor during the Nazi regime. As a priest in Communist Poland, he lived under the constant surveillance of authorities working to undermine the Church in Poland. And yet, the surrounding darkness did not prevent him from blossoming as a priest and from becoming a channel of grace that helped turn the tide of history in the most unexpected ways.

Inspired by John Paul II's first visit to his homeland in 1979, some fifty million Roman Catholics in eastern Europe—including thirty million in Poland and more than four million in the Soviet Union—were drawn together in peaceful protest to bring an end to the Cold War and to Communism in Europe. The Solidarity model of nonviolent resistance—the building of an extensive network of workers and intellectuals, combined with the weight of moral authority—turned out to be the answer to Stalin's mocking question, "The pope? And how many divisions does the pope have?"

John Paul II himself refused to take the credit for his part in the end of the Cold War: "I didn't cause it to happen. . . . The tree was already rotten. I just gave it a good shake and the rotten apples fell."[12] He attributed it, instead, to the work of the Holy Spirit in the life of the Church and the world, a subject he reflected on in his fifth encyclical letter, *Dominum et Vivificantem* (Lord and Giver of Life), issued on May 18, 1986.

Questions for personal reflection and faith sharing:

🕭 How do I wish to be radically transformed by the Holy Spirit?

🕭 Isaiah 11:2 identifies the gifts of the Holy Spirit as wisdom, understanding, counsel, fortitude, knowledge, piety, and fear of the Lord. What gifts has the Holy Spirit instilled in me or called me to receive? How is God calling me to share these gifts with others?

🕭 In what ways have I seen the Holy Spirit's work in my own church community, in the universal Church, in the world today, or in a historic event? How may the Holy Spirit be calling me to participate in this work?

Guidance for prayer and action:

🕭 Develop the habit of frequently praising and thanking the "sweet guest of your soul," as the Holy Spirit is often called. Call upon him for direction, strength, and inspiration before you begin your day and before every endeavor. Pray, "*Veni Sancte Spiritus* (Come, Holy Spirit)."

🕭 Consider participating in any of the new ecclesial movements and communities in the Church that meet regularly for prayer, Scripture study, and faith sharing. John Paul II looked upon these movements as a "providential answer" of the Holy Spirit for the

Church today, as they help people from all walks of life rediscover Pentecost as a living reality in their lives. (A list of some of
these movements and communities is contained in the *Directory
of Lay Movements, Organizations, and Professional Associations*
published by the United States Conference of Catholic Bishops.
A similar directory has been published by the Pontifical Council
for the Laity.)

❦ Prayerfully read John Paul II's encyclical letter *Dominum
et Vivificantem* (Lord and Giver of Life), and his catechesis
on the gifts of the Holy Spirit, given in the following series of
Regina Caeli and *Angelus* messages: the Gift of Wisdom (April
9, 1989); the Gift of Understanding (April 16, 1989); the Gift
of Knowledge (April 23, 1989); the Gift of Counsel (May 7,
1989); the Gift of Fortitude (May 14, 1989); the Gift of Piety
(May 28, 1989); the Gift of Fear of the Lord (June 11, 1989).
These reflections can be found at www.vatican.va/liturgical_year/
pentecost/2004/pentecoste_en.html# under the heading "On the
Holy Spirit."

❦ Reflect upon how the fruits of the Spirit—love, joy, peace,
patience, kindness, goodness, faithfulness, gentleness, self-
control (Galatians 5:22-25)—have grown in your life. Focus on
each fruit and ask yourself "Am I growing in love and charity for
God and neighbor? Do I live in joy? Do I have the peace that this
world cannot give? Am I patient in all circumstances? Do I treat
everyone I encounter with kindness and gentleness? Am I faithful
in all my relationships? Do I exercise self-control when tempted

to sin?" Reflect upon the aspects of the Spirit's fruits that need to grow in your life. If, for instance, you have an inclination to be unnecessarily anxious to the point of being robbed of your inner peace, consistently pray for the Holy Spirit to transform this anxiety into peace and trust in the Lord. Be mindful of the growth of true peace within you in specific situations, and thank the Holy Spirit for his aid. Offer to God whatever difficulties you may be having, and bring them to the Sacrament of Reconciliation.

❧ Pick a Scripture verse that talks about a virtue that you would like to strengthen. If, for instance, you have a tendency to be restless in prayer, meditate on a verse such as; "Be still before the LORD, and wait patiently for him" (Psalm 37:7). (A biblical topical concordance is very helpful for finding appropriate verses.)

❧ When reflecting upon current events, pray for the grace to see how the Holy Spirit is working to renew the face of the earth. Seek the Church's perspective on these events by subscribing to a Catholic news service and by seeking the views of writers who present modern-day issues in the light of Church teachings.

❧ Pray a novena to the Holy Spirit on the nine days prior to Pentecost. John Paul II highlights the importance of praying a novena during this time. He said, "Let us try to reflect deeply . . . and in a certain way to enter the Upper Room together with Mary and with the Apostles, preparing our souls to accept the Holy Spirit and his action in us. All this is of great importance for the interior maturity of our faith, of our Christian vocation."[13]

GOD'S WORD

"If you love me, you will keep my commandments. And I will pray the Father, and he will give you another Counselor, to be with you for ever, even the Spirit of truth, whom the world cannot receive, because it neither sees him nor knows him; you know him, for he dwells with you, and will be in you."

—John 14:15-17

Closing prayer: Come, Spirit of love and peace! Creator Spirit, hidden builder of the kingdom, by the power of your saints guide the Church to carry to the coming generations the light of the Word who brings salvation. Spirit of holiness, divine breath which moves the universe, come and renew the face of the earth.[14]

1. John Paul II, General Audience, May 30, 1979, 2.
2. John Paul II, May 30, 1979, 3.
3. John Paul II, Homily, Mass in Victory Square, Warsaw, June 2, 1979, 4.
4. Bogdan Szajkowski, quoted in Jane Barnes and Helen Whitney, "John Paul II and the Fall of Communism," *Frontline*, PBS, September 28, 1999.
5. George Wiegel, quoted in Barnes and Whitney.
6. Wojciech Jaruzelski, quoted in Barnes and Whitney.
7. Lech Walesa, quoted in "What World Leaders Say about Pope John Paul II," Zenit News Agency, April 10, 2005.

8. John Kwitney, *Man of the Century* (New York: Henry Holt & Company, Inc., 1997), p. 592.

9. Jaruzelski, quoted in Barnes and Whitney.

10. John Paul II, Meeting with Ecclesial Movements and New Communities, May 30, 1998, 4.

11. John Paul II, Encyclical Letter *Dominum et Vivificantem* (On the Holy Spirit in the Life of the Church and the World), May 18, 1986, 67.

12. John Paul II, quoted in Carl Bernstein and Marco Politi, *His Holiness* (New York: Doubleday, 1996), p. 356.

13. John Paul II, May 30, 1979, 2.

14. Adapted from John Paul II's prayer to the Holy Spirit in preparation for the Great Jubilee.

The Church of the Eucharist

Theme: The Eucharist is the source of life, of growth, and the unity in the Church.

Opening prayer: Dear Lord, we thank you for giving your Church her greatest treasure, your own body and blood, soul and divinity in the Eucharist. We pray that as you offer your life to us in the Blessed Sacrament, we too may offer our lives as a gift of love to you and to our brothers and sisters in Christ. As you choose to make yourself known to us in the breaking of the bread, we pray for the grace to always recognize you in the heavenly bread that gives us life. May we always know that heaven unites with earth when we receive you in the Eucharist.

ABOUT JOHN PAUL II

Holy Thursday, which celebrates Christ's institution of the Eucharist, was always a special day for John Paul II. It was a day in which the Church honors, in a special way, the Eucharist and the priesthood. Every year on Holy Thursday, Pope John Paul II sent a special letter to all the priests throughout the world. Then in the twenty-fifth year of his pontificate, he issued what would be his last encyclical, *Ecclesia de Eucharistia* (The Church of the Eucharist), as a way of both thanking the Lord for the gift of the Eucharist and the priesthood and emphasizing the centrality of the Eucharist in the life of the Church and the world.

When reflecting upon the meaning of the Eucharist in his own life as a priest, the Holy Father recalled that every day, beginning on November 2, 1946, when he celebrated his first Mass in the crypt of Saint Leonard in the Wawel Cathedral in Krakow, he experienced a dramatic inner change as he gazed upon the host and chalice during the consecration. In some way, time and space seemed to "merge," and the drama of Golgotha came alive in the present. Each day, he was "able to recognize in the consecrated bread and wine the divine Wayfarer who joined the two disciples on the road to Emmaus and opened their eyes to the light and their hearts to new hope (Luke 24:13-35)."[1]

Celebrating Mass in a great variety of locales—in churches throughout the world, in chapels built along mountain paths, on lake shores and seacoasts, on altars built in stadiums and in city squares, or even at a hospital bedside—led John Paul II to see the Eucharist as more than just a local celebration. "This varied scenario of celebrations of the Eucharist," he explained, "has given me a powerful experience of its universal and, so to speak, cosmic character. Yes, cosmic! Because even when it is celebrated on the humble altar of a country church, the Eucharist is always in some way celebrated *on the altar of the world.* It unites heaven and earth. It embraces and permeates all creation."[2]

In *Ecclesia de Eucharistia*, John Paul II invites us to contemplate the Blessed Sacrament as the heart of the Church's mystery, the source of life, of growth, and of unity in the Church from its very beginnings—truly the "source and summit of the Christian life." He invites us to enlist the aid of his and our mother, "the Woman of the Eucharist," who conceived the Son of God in the physical reality of his body and blood. As the tabernacle of the new covenant, she anticipated within herself "what to some degree happens sacramentally in every believer who receives, under the signs of bread and wine, the Lord's body and blood."[3] In receiving the Eucharist, we find that our life, like Mary's, finds its true meaning and purpose in being one with Christ.

Pause: How can I be a more worthy tabernacle of the Lord?

JOHN PAUL II's WORDS

The Church has received the Eucharist from Christ her Lord not as one gift—however precious—among so many others, but as the gift par excellence, for it is the gift of himself, of his person in his sacred humanity, as well as the gift of his saving work. Nor does it remain confined to the past, since "all that Christ is—all that he did and suffered for all men—participates in the divine eternity, and so transcends all times."

When the Church celebrates the Eucharist, the memorial of her Lord's death and resurrection, this central event of salvation becomes really present and "the work of our redemption is carried out." This sacrifice is so decisive for the salvation of the human race that Jesus Christ offered it and returned to the Father only after he had left us a means of sharing in it as if we had been present there.

Each member of the faithful can thus take part in it and inexhaustibly gain its fruits. This is the faith from which generations of Christians down the ages have lived.[4]

In the Eucharist we have Jesus, we have his redemptive sacrifice, we have his resurrection, we have the gift of the Holy Spirit, we have adoration, obedience, and love of the Father. Were we to disregard the Eucharist, how could we overcome our own deficiency?[5]

In the humble signs of bread and wine, changed into his body and blood, Christ walks beside us as our strength and our food for the journey, and he enables us to become, for everyone, witnesses of hope. If, in the presence of this mystery, reason experiences its limits, the heart, enlightened by the grace of the Holy Spirit, clearly sees the response that is demanded, and bows low in adoration and unbounded love.[6]

REFLECTION

When Jesus said, "He who eats my flesh and drinks my blood abides in me, and I in him" (John 6:56), many of his disciples drew back and no longer wanted to be with him. Throughout the ages since Jesus spoke those words, faith in the Real Presence—the body and blood, soul and divinity of our Lord Jesus Christ actually present in the Holy Eucharist—has remained the constant teaching of the Church. For more than two thousand years, the Church has drawn her life from the Eucharist, and yet, to this day, many still draw back from Christ's words.

In responding to the Holy Father's invitation to more deeply contemplate the eucharistic face of Christ, we too may find ourselves unable to grasp this reality that far exceeds the limits of our senses and our intellect. But in the humble act of receiving Jesus as he wishes to give himself to us, we let God be God, and we allow ourselves to be consumed by his love for us.

Questions for personal reflection and faith sharing:

❧ What teaching of John Paul II about the Eucharist can I take into prayer and contemplation? In what ways might this help my journey of faith?

❧ How has the Holy Eucharist nourished my life? How do I encounter Christ's real presence in the Blessed Sacrament?

❧ What can I share with others about my personal experience of the Eucharist that would serve to strengthen their faith in Christ's real presence?

Guidance for prayer and action:

❧ Make your daily examination of conscience a sincere and thorough preparation to receive Jesus in the Eucharist. Ask the Holy Spirit to search you and help you prepare to receive the Eucharist in a worthy manner, for "whoever, therefore, eats the bread or drinks the cup of the Lord in an unworthy manner will be guilty of profaning the body and blood of the Lord" (1 Corinthians 11:27). Know the peace that comes from being fully reconciled with God through the Sacrament of Reconciliation, which prepares us for full participation in the eucharistic sacrifice.

☙ Before Mass, ask the Holy Spirit for the grace—for you and for all your brothers and sisters around you—to become profoundly aware of your integral part in the celebration. As John Paul II reminds us, "In the Eucharist the Church is completely united to Christ and his sacrifice."[7] Far from being spectators in the pews, we are joined in Christ in a sacred offering of our lives to God. In this offering, God fills us with his Spirit and sends us, transformed, back into the world.

☙ Read and treasure in your heart these New Testament passages about the Eucharist: John 6:52-71; Mark 14:22-25; 1 Corinthians: 10:14-17; 1 Corinthians 11:23-32; Matthew 26:1-2, 26-28; Luke 22:14-22, 24:30-35. Then ponder these Old Testament passages that prefigure the Eucharist (Exodus 12:1-3; 12:21-28).

☙ Read the eucharistic writings of the early Church Fathers. Ignatius of Antioch, for example, in his epistle to the Smyrneans (c. 100), spoke of "those who hold strange doctrines. . . . They abstain from the Eucharist and from prayer, because they confess not the Eucharist to be flesh of our Savior Jesus Christ."[8] Similarly, Justin Martyr (c. 152) emphasized the apostolic origins of the Eucharist, saying, "We have been taught that the food which is blessed by the prayer of His word, and from which our blood and flesh by transmutation are nourished, is the flesh and blood of that Jesus who was made flesh."[9] And Irenaeus—who was the disciple of Polycarp, himself a disciple of the apostle John—wrote (c. 185), "For as the bread, which is produced from the earth, when it receives the invocation of God, is no longer common bread, but the Eucharist, consisting of two realities, earthly and heavenly."[10]

❧ Stay close to Jesus in eucharistic adoration. As John Paul II tells us, "It is pleasant to spend time with him, to lie close to his breast like the Beloved Disciple (John 13:25) and to feel the infinite love present in his heart. . . . How often, dear brothers and sisters, have I experienced this, and drawn from it strength, consolation, and support!"[11]

GOD'S WORD

The Jews then disputed among themselves, saying, "How can this man give us his flesh to eat?" So Jesus said to them, "Truly, truly, I say to you, unless you eat the flesh of the Son of man and drink his blood, you have no life in you; he who eats my flesh and drinks my blood has eternal life, and I will raise him up at the last day. For my flesh is food indeed, and my blood is drink indeed. He who eats my flesh and drinks my blood abides in me, and

I in him. As the living Father sent me, and I live because of the Father, so he who eats me will live because of me. This is the bread which came down from heaven, not such as the fathers ate and died; he who eats this bread will live for ever."

—John 6:52-58

Closing prayer: "We thank you, our Father, for the life and the knowledge which you have revealed to us through Jesus, your servant. Glory to you through the ages! As the bread we have broken was scattered far and wide upon the hills, but when harvested becomes one, so may the Church be gathered into your Kingdom from the farthest reaches of the earth. . . . Lord almighty, you created the universe for the glory of your name; you gave men food and drink to strengthen them, that they might give you thanks; but to us you have given spiritual food and drink, and eternal life through your Son. . . . Glory to you through the ages."[12] Amen.

1. John Paul II, Encyclical Letter *Ecclesia de Eucharistia* (The Church of the Eucharist), April 17, 2003, 59.

2. John Paul II, *Ecclesia de Eucharistia*, 8.

3. John Paul II, *Ecclesia de Eucharistia*, 55.

4. John Paul II, *Ecclesia de Eucharistia*, 11.

5. John Paul II, *Ecclesia de Eucharistia*, 60.

6. John Paul II, *Ecclesia de Eucharistia*, 62.

7. John Paul II, *Ecclesia de Eucharistia*, 58.

8. Ignatius of Antioch, Epistle to the Smyrnaeans, 6.7.
9. Justin Martyr, First Apology, 66.2.
10. Ireneaus, Against Heresies, 4.18.5.
11. John Paul II, *Ecclesia de Eucharistia*, 25.
12. *Didache*, 9:3–4; 10:3–4. Pope John Paul II ended his *Letter to Priests* with this ancient prayer from the *Didache* on Holy Thursday 2000, the day he celebrated Mass in the Upper Room in Jerusalem, where Jesus celebrated the first Eucharist with his apostles. The *Didache* (Doctrine of the Twelve Apostles), written at the close of the first century or early in the second, is a short treatise that was accounted by some of the Church Fathers as next to Scripture in importance in the teaching of the faith.

Mary, Our Mother

Theme: The Blessed Mother is our model and guide for perfect discipleship.

Opening prayer: Lord Jesus, we thank you for giving your Church a mother, your very own mother. As you entrusted your incarnation to her, let us entrust ourselves to the care that you give us through her maternal love. Let us behold her as you behold her, and let us cherish her for the role that you have given her to play in our lives. Help us to always look to her as the one who has gone before us in our journey to our heavenly home with you.

ABOUT JOHN PAUL II

Totus Tuus, which translates "All yours," was the motto of John Paul II's papacy. Emblazoned on his papal coat of arms, this phrase comes from St. Louis Grignon de Montfort, an eighteenth-century priest whose devotion to the Blessed Mother had a profound influence on Karol Wojtyla. It is an abbreviation of a more detailed form of entrustment to the Mother of God: "*Totus Tuus ego sum et omnia mea Tua sunt. Accipio Te in mea omnia. Praebe mighi cor Tuum, Maria.* (I am all yours, and all I have is yours. I welcome you into all my affairs and concerns. Show me your heart, O Mary)." This phrase, as John Paul II said, is not only an expression of piety or devotion; it is, in fact, a consecration of one's life to "do whatever he tells you" (John 2:5).

As a young man, Karol Wojtyla thought that he ought to "distance" himself from the various devotions to Mary he had encountered as a boy in order to "focus more on Christ." Yet, his attitude changed during World War II, when, during idle hours on the late-night shift in the Solvay chemical plant, he read various works of St. Louis de Monfort, such as *Love of the Eternal Wisdom, Treatise on True Devotion to the Blessed Virgin*, and *The Secret of the Rosary*. Through these classics, Karol learned that authentic Marian piety always led beyond Mary to a much deeper relationship with Christ. Mary's fiat, "Let it be to me according to your word" (Luke 1:38), prepared the way for the discipleship of others. To be Christ's disciple was to be like Mary, who was utterly disposed to the will of God.

John Paul II's writings on the Blessed Mother contemplate her role in salvation history and in the life of the Church. In his encyclical letter *Redemptoris Mater* (Mother of the Redeemer), he considers the Blessed Mother's precise place in the plan of salvation, as well as her active and exemplary presence in the life of the Church. In his apostolic letter on the rosary, *Rosarium Virginis Mariae*, he describes the rosary as a Christocentric prayer that echoes Mary's perennial *Magnificat*: "With the rosary, the Christian people sits at the school of Mary and is led to contemplate the beauty of the face of Christ and to experience the depths of his love."[1] In order to bring out the Christological depth of the rosary, he proposed the addition of five mysteries, called the Mysteries of Light, which focus on Jesus' public ministry and help us to contemplate the mystery of Christ as the "light of the world" (John 8:12).[2]

In both his encyclical letter *Mulieris Dignitatem* (On the Dignity of Women) and his *Letter to Women*, in which Mary figures prominently, John Paul II dealt with the confusion and debate about the role of women in the family and the world today. For her total surrender to the will of God and for her role in the incarnation, he referred to Mary as the fullest expression of the "feminine genius." In wholeheartedly following Christ, John Paul II said, every woman, like Mary, can discover her femininity's deepest meaning and fulfillment. "After all," he wrote, "was it not in and through her that the greatest event in human history—the incarnation of God himself—was accomplished?"[3]

Pause: How can my relationship with Mary help deepen my relationship with Christ?

JOHN PAUL II'S WORDS

"From that hour the disciple took her to his own home" (John 19:27). Can the same be said of us? Do we also welcome Mary into our homes? Indeed, we should grant her full rights in the home of our lives, of our faith, of our affections, of our commitments, and acknowledge the maternal role that is hers, that is to say, her function as guide, as adviser, as encourager, or even merely as a silent presence, which at times may of itself be enough to infuse us with strength and courage. . . . [T]he first disciples, after

Jesus' ascension, were gathered with "Mary, the Mother of Jesus" (Acts 1:14). . . . The fact that she is specified as "the Mother of Jesus," shows how closely she was linked to the figure of her Son. It tells us that Mary recalls always the salvific value of the work of Jesus, our only Savior. On the other hand it likewise tells us that to believe in Jesus Christ cannot dispense us from including also in our act of faith the one who was his mother. In God's family, Mary watches over the diversity of each one within the communion among all. At the same time she can teach us to be open to the Holy Spirit, to share anxiously in Christ's total dedication to the will of the Father and, above all, to participate deeply in the passion of the Son and live our life and ministry with assured spiritual fruitfulness. "Behold, your mother!" (John 19:27). Everyone feels that these words are addressed to him and therefore draws faith and enthusiasm from them for an always more determined and serene journey along the committed road of one's own life.[4]

REFLECTION

From its earliest beginnings, the Church has been profoundly aware of the honor we must give to Mary, who is the Mother of God. While Scripture and sacred tradition have taught about the Blessed Mother's role not only in the life of the Church but also in the life of the world, John Paul II has faced the great challenge of upholding the Church's Marian teachings in his ecumenical dialogues.

The Church has always taught that our devotion to Mary in no way impedes our union with Christ; rather, it fosters that union. All the saving influences from Mary originate from God's divine pleasure and draw all their power from Christ.[5] As the pope explained, "This saving influence is sustained by the Holy Spirit, who, just as he overshadowed the Virgin Mary when he began in her the divine motherhood, in a similar way constantly sustains her solicitude for the brothers and sisters of her Son."[6]

John Paul II exhorts the Church to faithfully live Christ's words, "Behold, thy mother!" in all their depth and fullness. We have a mother in heaven who loves us and cares for us. In her complete, unquestioning surrender to God's will, she is the perfect model of discipleship. Let us ask the Holy Spirit for the grace to behold the Mother of God as our very own.

Questions for personal reflection and faith sharing:

❧ How would I describe my relationship with the Blessed Mother? Have my family and I welcomed her into our home, to love and honor her as the apostle John did?

❧ What have I learned from John Paul II about the value and appropriateness of devotion to Mary for my spiritual growth?

❧ Have I had any encounters with the Blessed Mother (in prayer, in Scripture, in a Marian pilgrimage) in which I felt her presence and her loving care? How can I share these experiences with others in a way that could help them in their spiritual journey?

❧ How do I see Mary as "the fulfillment of the feminine genius"? What qualities in a woman express authentic femininity?

Guidance for prayer and action:

❧ In meditation, place yourself with Mary at the foot of the cross where Christ, her son, is suffering and dying. Unite your heart with hers. The man on the cross is the fruit of her womb, the baby she nursed, loved, disciplined, and watched as he grew into the fullness of his manhood. He is the young man who turned water into wine at her request. Every drop of his blood is precious to her. The reality of his pain and suffering pierces her heart. Yet, like Jesus in his agony in the garden, she says, "Yes, Father, be it done according to your will." Spend some time with Mary in her solitude after her son's death. Contemplate the deep inner peace that she must have felt with the Father in spite of her sorrow.

❧ Continue your meditation with Mary as she buries her son in the tomb and returns to Jerusalem with John. Witness Mary in the Upper Room with the apostles and other disciples who, frightened and confused, have returned seeking refuge and the company of their intimate companions. Notice how Mary, even though her heart is filled with grief, comforts them—how, with tender motherly love, she shares her peace, faith, and hope with them. Rest awhile in the corner of the room and dwell on Mary as the comforter, the one who gives only the love that her son gives. End your meditation with the Lord's Prayer.

❧ Pray the rosary individually, as a family, or as a group, even when you can only manage to find time to pray a decade. John Paul II repeatedly encouraged individuals and families to pray the rosary: "It could be said that each mystery of the Rosary, carefully meditated, sheds light on the mystery of man. At the same time, it becomes natural to bring to this encounter with the sacred humanity of the Redeemer all the problems, anxieties, labors, and endeavors which go to make up our lives. 'Cast your burden on the Lord and he will sustain you' (Psalm 55:23). To pray the Rosary is to hand over our burdens to the merciful hearts of Christ and his Mother."[7]

❧ Read about Church-approved apparitions of the Blessed Mother or go on a pilgrimage to a Marian shrine or apparition site. Find a list of these apparitions at www.marypages.com. Our Lady of Fatima holds special significance in the life of Pope John Paul II, for he attributed his survival of an assassination attempt in 1981 to her divine intervention.

❧ Do something special to honor the mothers in your life. If your own mother, grandmother, or godmother is still alive, send her a token of your appreciation, such as a note or flowers. If she is deceased, have a Mass said for her, and tell your own children or other family members what she was like.

GOD'S WORD

And Mary said,
"My soul magnifies the Lord,
  and my spirit rejoices in God my Savior,
for he has regarded the low estate of his
    handmaiden.
  For behold, henceforth all generations will call
    me blessed;
for he who is mighty has done great things for me,
    and holy is his name.
And his mercy is on those who fear him
    from generation to generation."

—Luke 1:46-50

Closing prayer: "Mary, woman clothed with the sun, help us to fix our gaze on Christ amid the inevitable sufferings and problems of everyday life. Help us to not be afraid of following him to the very end, even when the cross seems unbearably heavy. Make us understand that this alone is the way which leads to the heights of eternal salvation. And from heaven, where you shine forth as Queen and Mother of mercy, watch over each one of your children. Guide [us] to love, adore, and serve Jesus, the blessed fruit of your womb, O clement, O loving, O sweet Virgin Mary!"[8]

1. John Paul II, Apostolic Letter *Rosarium Virginis Mariae* (On the Most Holy Rosary), October 16, 2002, 1.
2. John Paul II, *Rosarium Virginis Mariae,* 19.
3. John Paul II, Apostolic Letter *Mulieris Dignitatem* (On the Dignity of Women), August 15, 1988, 31.
4. John Paul II, Homily, First International Congress of the Focolare Movement, April 30, 1982, 5.
5. Vatican Council II, *Lumen Gentium* (Dogmatic Constitution on the Church), November 21, 1964, 60.
6. John Paul II, Encyclical Letter *Redemptoris Mater* (Mother of the Redeemer), March 25, 1987, 38.
7. John Paul II, *Rosarium Virginis Mariae,* 25.
8. John Paul II, Homily on the Solemnity of the Assumption, August 15, 1997, 4.

MEDITATION SIX
The Gospel of Life

Theme: "Respect, protect, love, and serve life, every human life! Only in this direction will you find justice, development, true freedom, peace, and happiness!"[1]

Opening prayer: Lord Jesus, we thank you for the gift of life, and for revealing to us the great mystery of life in all its glory. Help us to behold every person we encounter as your own beloved, a person of infinite worth and dignity. Grant us the grace to always love and care for every person you entrust to us, and to defend the life of the unborn, the poor, the persecuted, the sick, and the elderly.

ABOUT JOHN PAUL II

In 1994 Pope John Paul II confronted a monumental challenge to his gospel of life in the global arena. The United Nations World Conference on Population and Development was scheduled to meet that year in Cairo. From the perspective of the Church, the draft documents prepared in advance of the conference were deeply troubling. Severing sexual expression from marriage and procreation, the conference's sponsors sought to define sexual expression as a freestanding personal right under international law. There was even a paragraph seeking to define a legally enforceable universal right to abortion on demand.

On March 19, 1994, John Paul II sent a letter to every head of state in the world and to the secretary-general of the United Nations. The letter expressed the Church's support for the UN's current International Year of the Family as well as for the "duty of civil authorities . . . to strive to promote the harmonious growth of the family." However, the pope pointed out that while development was to be the co-theme of the conference, development issues had been "almost completely overlooked." Instead, as he stated, the draft document was far more interested in promoting a "totally individualistic" idea of human sexuality to the extent that "marriage now appears as something outmoded." This he found more than ironic, noting that the Universal Declaration of Human Rights contained in the document clearly stated that the family was "the natural and fundamental group unit of society." Vatican spokesman Joaquin Navarro-Valls recalls the pope's reaction to paragraph 8.25, the statement about abortion: "He feared that for the first time in the history of humanity, abortion was being proposed as a means of population control. He put all the prestige of his office at the service of this issue."[2]

During the conference's sessions—attended by representatives from 185 nations, including the Holy See—the pope kept in constant touch with his delegation from Rome. He also mounted a passionate but carefully reasoned appeal in the court of world opinion. It consisted of twelve widely publicized ten-minute addresses at his weekly general audience or the Sunday Angelus. The first of these stressed the right to life as the basic human right and the foundation of any meaningful platform for human rights. His succeeding addresses dealt with the sanctity of marriage and human sexuality, authentic feminism, the public dimensions of the abortion issue, and the dehumanizing effects of radical individualism. He rejected coercive family planning programs as violations of a married couple's basic human rights and rejected artificial contraception as a violation of God's design for human sexual love. At the same time, he reminded the world that the Church does not teach an "ideology of fertility at all costs," but responsible family planning through the natural method of periodic abstinence.

That year, *Time* magazine selected John Paul II as its "Man of the Year." Referring to the Cairo conference, the magazine stated, simply, "The pope won." One sign of his victory was the insertion of an explicit statement that "in no case should abortion be promoted as a method of family planning." *Time*'s editorial concluded, "The Man of the Year's ideas about what can be accomplished differ from those of most mortals. They are far grander, informed by a vision as vast as the human determination to bring them into being. After discovering the principle of the lever and the fulcrum in the third century B.C., Archimedes wrote, 'Give me where to stand, and I will move the earth.' John Paul knows where he stands."[3]

Pause: How does John Paul II's witness to the gospel of life challenge and inspire me to proclaim, celebrate, and defend life?

JOHN PAUL II's WORDS

In [the] great endeavor to create a new culture of life, we are inspired and sustained by the confidence that comes from knowing that the Gospel of life, like the Kingdom of God itself, is growing and producing abundant fruit (Mark 4:26-29). There is certainly an enormous disparity between the powerful resources available to the forces promoting the "culture of death" and the means at the disposal of those working for a "culture of life and love." But we know that we can rely on the help of God, for whom nothing is impossible (Matthew 19:26).

Filled with this certainty, and moved by profound concern for the destiny of every man and woman, I repeat what I said to those families who carry out their challenging mission amid so many difficulties: a great prayer for life is urgently needed, a prayer which will rise up throughout the world. Through special initiatives and in daily prayer, may an impassioned plea rise to God, the Creator and lover of life, from every Christian community, from every group and association, from every family, and from the heart of every believer. Jesus himself has shown us by his own example that prayer and fasting are the first and most effective weapons against the forces of evil (Matthew 4:1-11). As he taught his disciples, some demons cannot be driven out except in this way (Mark 9:29). Let us therefore discover anew the humility and the courage to pray and fast so that power from on high will break down the walls of lies and deceit: the walls which conceal from the sight of so many of our brothers and sisters the evil of practices and laws which are hostile to life. May this same power turn their hearts to resolutions and goals inspired by the civilization of life and love.[4]

REFLECTION

The mission of the Church has always been to protect and nurture human life: to care for the poor, heal the sick, and spread the gospel message of eternal life. Yet, while it has often experienced difficulties in fulfilling this mission, today the Church faces the unprecedented challenge of convincing the world of the dignity and sanctity of human life in an atmosphere where life is often considered cheap and expendable. While our present-day society has developed an increasing sensitivity to human rights, it has not succeeded in applying them to the defense of those who are most vulnerable—the unborn, the sick, and the elderly.

In addition to the millions of abortions performed worldwide each year, other assaults on human life, including infanticide, euthanasia, and destructive experimentation on human embryos, are increasing. Unfortunately, they are often claimed to be rights based on individual freedom; there is a trend toward their recognition in law; and they are carried out with the help of medical science. It is in this historical context that Pope John Paul II accepted the invitation of the College of Cardinals to write an encyclical that reflects upon and gives voice to the Christian response to the intensifying "culture of death."

After four years of drafting *Evangelium Vitae* (Gospel of Life) in close consultation with every bishop in the world, John Paul II signed the encyclical on the feast of the Annunciation, March 25, 1995. He called it "a document that I consider central to the whole of the Magisterium of my pontificate."[5] Others have called it a new Magna Carta, a charter that guides those who wish to help build the culture of life by bringing the love of Christ to the weak and the helpless.

Questions for personal reflection and faith sharing:

&. When and how did I first become aware of the clash between the culture of death and the culture of life? How has my awareness of this conflict affected the way that I look upon and treat the unborn, the poor, the sick, the elderly, and those on death row?

&. How have I experienced and witnessed the power of prayer and fasting as the most effective weapons in overcoming the forces behind the culture of death?

&. Do I know any person or community in which the gospel of life is lived in an extraordinary way? What is it about this person or community that is so special, and that moves me to live the gospel of life more deeply?

&. Reflect upon the following statement by John Paul II on the death penalty: "A sign of hope is the increasing recognition that the dignity of life must never be taken away, even in the case of someone who has done great evil. Modern society has the means of protecting itself, without definitively denying criminals the chance to reform."[6]

Guidance for prayer and action:

❧ Contemplate your own life in your mother's womb and how, from the moment of conception, God created you to know his love, to love, and to be loved. What if you were not given the chance to live? Spend more time in silence contemplating the life you would not have had if you were one of the millions who died in abortion. Praise and thank God for your own birth and for all the love that it took for you to be alive today.

❧ Pray daily for an end to abortion. Pray for anyone you know who is considering an abortion. With other members of your church, plan for a special day (or days) of prayer and fasting every year for the express purpose of putting an end to the culture of death in all its manifestations.

❧ Ask the Holy Spirit to show you how you can more fully share your life and your love with the unborn, the poor, the persecuted, the sick, and the elderly. Ask him to give you hope and confidence that you can make a difference in building a culture of life through simple acts of kindness and love. End with the Lord's Prayer.

❧ Consider your attitudes and past behaviors with regard to respect-for-life issues. Are there any errors of omission or commission that need to be addressed? Seek guidance and help if necessary.

❧ Extend God's love and mercy to women who have had abortions. Tell them about the healing ministries that the Church offers to them. (Contact your diocese to get information on these ministries.) Give them a copy of paragraph 99 in John Paul II's encyclical *Evangelium Vitae,* which is a compassionate message to women who have had an abortion.

❧ Volunteer at your local crisis pregnancy center, and learn how to counsel and help women who are considering an abortion.

❧ Stay informed about abortion and other life issues. Whenever important life issues come into the public eye, write to your local newspaper, to your elected officials, and to others whose actions and policies may be influenced by your voice. Make an ardent plea for compassionate justice and respect for life. Speak up with courage and charity in defense of those who are weak and incapable of defending themselves.

❧ Take part in respectful pro-life activities. Perhaps you could join with others in praying the rosary in front of your local abortion clinic or a death-row facility.

God's Word

For thou didst form my inward parts,
    thou didst knit me together in my mother's
    womb.
I praise thee, for thou art fearful and wonderful.
    Wonderful are thy works!
Thou knowest me right well;
    my frame was not hidden from thee,
when I was being made in secret,
    intricately wrought in the depths of the earth.
Thy eyes beheld my unformed substance;
    in thy book were written, every one of them,
the days that were formed for me,
    when as yet there was none of them.

                      —Psalm 139:13-16

Closing prayer: "O Mary, bright dawn of the new world, Mother of the living, to you do we entrust the cause of life: Look down, O Mother, upon the vast numbers of babies not allowed to be born, of the poor whose lives are made difficult, of men and women who are victims of brutal violence, of the elderly and the sick killed by indifference or out of misguided mercy. Grant that all who believe in your Son may proclaim the Gospel of life with honesty and love to the people of our time. Obtain for them the grace to accept that Gospel as a gift ever new, the joy of celebrating it with gratitude throughout their lives and the courage to bear witness to it resolutely, in order to build, together with all people of good will, the civilization of truth and love, to the praise and glory of God, the Creator and lover of life."[7] Amen.

1. John Paul II, Encyclical Letter *Evangelium Vitae* (On the Value and Inviolability of Human Life), March 25, 1995, 5.
2. Gray, Paul, "Man of the Year: Empire of the Spirit," *Time*, December 26, 1994, p. 56.
3. Gray, p. 57.
4. John Paul II, *Evangelium Vitae*, 100.
5. John Paul II, Papal Discourse on the 5th Anniversary of *Evangelium Vitae*, February 14, 2000, 1.
6. John Paul II, Homily, Mass in the Trans World Dome, St. Louis, January 27, 1999, 5.
7. John Paul II, *Evangelium Vitae*, 105.

MEDITATION SEVEN

Aging in Grace

Theme: Faith brings serenity to old age and illuminates the mystery of death.

Opening prayer: Father in heaven, we thank you for giving us your beloved Son, who has given us the gift to see our lives in the perspective of eternity. Let us never lose sight of the unfading youthfulness of the soul you have given us, especially amid the physical trials the flesh may bring in our twilight years. Grant us the grace to serve you and your beloved children, in prayer and in charity, to the very end. Help us to look forward, with great joy and gratitude, to the time when you will call us home to you.

ABOUT JOHN PAUL II

When Karol Wojtyla was elected pope, he was an active, robust fifty-seven-year-old man. In the early years of his papacy, he was an avid sportsman, a tireless globetrotter, and a powerful speaker. Toward the end of his life, however, the ravages of old age, Parkinson's disease, and past injuries made every step difficult and every word a labor. Many wondered if he could continue to perform his duties as pope; some suggested that he ought to retire. Yet John Paul II firmly believed that he had to continue serving God and the Church as pope until his dying day, and that even his frailty and illness could serve a purpose in God's design. As he continued to appear before the world with his hands in constant tremor, his speech slurred, and his body bent in pain and fatigue, many people were inspired and empowered by his example to serve to the very end.

It was not without difficulty that John Paul II had come to accept the realities of old age. After he fell in his bathtub and injured his leg in April of 1994, he realized that he would never walk again without pain and effort. During a brief vacation that summer in the mountains of Val D'Aosta, the pope's friend and student Father Tadeusz Styczen noted that John Paul II seemed to agonize over his condition. Yet by the end of the week, Styczen remembered, "John Paul II had passed through this particular dark night, come to grips with his new situation, and was renewed in his resolve to carry on his mission."[1]

Four and a half years later, on October 1, 1999, the seventy-nine-year-old pontiff issued his *Letter to the Elderly*. In this deeply personal letter, he expressed his spiritual closeness to those in their later years by reflecting upon the gift of old age and the vital role of older people in society.

John Paul II's last years were some of the most active of his life. He continued to feed and strengthen his flock as he celebrated the sacraments, ordained priests, wrote papal documents and books, made pastoral visits abroad, canonized saints, met with world leaders, attended his last World Youth Day gathering, and shared meals with the poor and homeless.[2] His last days were marked with a sustained desire to be close to his flock in prayer, as he suffered the complications of various illnesses. On the eve of his death, the pope was "conscious and serene" as he concelebrated Mass from his bed and listened to the Stations of the Cross and the reading of the Divine Office. At around 3:30 p.m. on April 2, 2005, the Holy Father's last words were, "Let me go to the Father's house." At 8:00 p.m. the Mass for the feast of Divine Mercy was celebrated at the foot of his bed, while only the light of a small candle illuminated the darkness of his apartment. Liturgical songs sung in the Mass blended with those of the multitude gathered in prayer in St. Peter's Square. At 9:37 p.m. the 264th pope departed this world and went home to the Lord.[3]

Pause: What is the most valuable lesson I can learn from John Paul II about living my elderly years and approaching my death?

JOHN PAUL II'S WORDS

Despite the limitations brought on by age, I continue to enjoy life. For this I thank the Lord. It is wonderful to be able to give oneself to the very end for the sake of the Kingdom of God! At the same time, I find great peace in thinking of the time when the Lord will call me: from life to life! And so I often find myself saying, with no trace of melancholy, a prayer recited by priests after the celebration of the Eucharist: "At the hour of my death, call me and bid me come to you." This is the prayer of Christian hope, which in no way detracts from the joy of the present, while entrusting the future to God's gracious and loving care."[4]

My thoughts turn in a special way to you, widows and widowers, who find yourselves alone in the final part of your lives; to you, elderly men and women religious, who for long years have faithfully served the cause of the Kingdom of Heaven; and to you, dear brother priests and bishops, who, for reasons of age, no longer have direct responsibility for pastoral ministry. The Church still needs you. She appreciates the services which you may wish to provide in many areas of the apostolate; she counts on the support of your longer periods of prayer; she counts on your advice born of experience, and she is enriched by your daily witness to the Gospel.[5]

The Christian community can receive much from the serene presence of older people. . . . There are many other areas where the elderly can make a beneficial contribution. The Spirit acts as and where he wills, and quite frequently he employs human means which seem of little account in the eyes of the world. How many people find understanding and comfort from elderly people who may be lonely or ill and yet are able to instill courage by their loving advice, their silent prayers, or their witness of suffering borne with patient acceptance! At the very time when their physical energies and their level of activity are decreasing, these brothers and sisters of ours become all the more precious in the mysterious plan of Providence.[6]

Reflection

In his *Letter to the Elderly,* John Paul II pointed out one of the great tragedies in our world today—the failure of many people to honor the preciousness of the elderly in God's plan. In the past, he noted, the elderly were held in great esteem and sought out for their wisdom and special contributions. These days, however, society tends to put a premium on the vigor and productivity of the young, while undervaluing the gifts and contributions of people who are older. As a result, many older people "themselves are led to wonder whether their lives are still worthwhile."[7]

John Paul II himself had to resist the prevailing views of society and firmly fix his gaze on God's will for his old age. While many thought that his physical infirmity was a clear sign that he should step down, he used it as an opportunity to call upon an inner strength that became all the more evident in physical weakness. In his younger days, many people attributed his appeal to his charisma, his boundless energy, and his immense creative output. When those gave way to frailty and illness, the world saw in the suffering pope a great lesson in how to live, as well as how to die—and that "the service of the Gospel has nothing to do with age!"[8] He showed us that such service can be rendered even when all we have left to offer to God are our sufferings and our frailty—and for this, our offering is all the more precious in God's eyes and in his divine plan. Moreover, he taught us to anchor our sights on eternity rather than on the fleeting joys and sorrows we experience in this world.

Questions for personal reflection and faith sharing:

❧ How can I make the senior years of my life most meaningful? How can I stay open to God's call to serve him in some special way in my old age?

❧ How can I share more of the wisdom I have gained in my lifetime with my family and with those who are younger than I am?

❧ How may God be calling me to more deeply honor and serve the elderly in my family and in my community?

❧ Do I look upon death with fear and aversion, or do I move toward it graciously, longing for the time when I will pass through life's threshold to eternity? If I am fearful, what can I do to overcome my fears?

Guidance for prayer and action:

❧ In his *Letter to the Elderly,* John Paul II portrays the senior years as a time to be used creatively to deepen our spiritual life through intensified prayer and service to others. In prayer, ask, "What would you have me do, Lord, to draw closer to you, to take better care of myself, and to serve you and my brothers and sisters throughout the remaining years of my life?" Go for a walk, engage in journaling, and spend time with the Lord before the Blessed Sacrament to discern his will in its fullness.

❧ John Paul II placed great importance on the role of the elderly as teachers of the faith. If you're a grandparent, take the time to talk about your relationship to God with your grandchildren, using stories from your own life that relate how your faith has strengthened and nourished you. Find some quiet time to write to your children and grandchildren about the important lessons you have learned and the precious insights you have gained over the years. This will be a spiritual legacy that they will truly treasure.

❧ Volunteer to help with your parish's youth group or to teach faith-formation classes to young people. Join or volunteer to lead an intergenerational faith-sharing group.

❧ Make a list of the many gifts God has given you, and take this list to Mass. During the offertory, say a quiet prayer offering these gifts to the Lord, and ask him where he wants you to use them in the service of the gospel. Meditate on any of the following Scripture passages: "Even to your old age I am He, and to gray hairs I will carry you. I have made, and I will bear; I will carry and will save" (Isaiah 46:4); "They still bring forth fruit in old age" (Psalm 92:14); "Let the elders who rule well be considered worthy of double honor, especially those who labor in preaching and teaching" (1 Timothy 5:17).

❧ Find out how you can support the elderly in your community, perhaps by providing transportation to Mass, bringing the Eucharist to the homebound, volunteering at a nursing center, or inviting elderly people to your family gatherings. Think of other ways to extend God's love and comfort to them.

GOD'S WORD

"I am the resurrection and the life; he who believes in me, though he die, yet shall he live, and whoever lives and believes in me shall never die."

—John 11:25-26

Closing Prayer: "Grant, O Lord of life, that we may . . . savor every season of our lives as a gift filled with promise for the future.

Grant that we may lovingly accept your will, and place ourselves each day in your merciful hands.

And when the moment of our definitive 'passage' comes, grant that we may face it with serenity, without regret for what we shall leave behind. . . .

Mary, Mother of pilgrim humanity, pray for us 'now and at the hour of our death.' Keep us ever close to Jesus, your beloved Son and our brother, the Lord of life and glory. Amen!"[9]

1. Weigel, *Witness to Hope,* p. 722.
2. Vatican Web site biography of John Paul II.
3. "John Paul II's Last Words: Vatican Publishes the Final 'Stations' of His Way of the Cross," Zenit News Agency, Sept. 21, 2005.

4. John Paul II, *Letter to the Elderly,* October 1, 1999, 17.

5. John Paul II, *Letter to the Elderly,* 13.

6. John Paul II, *Letter to the Elderly,* 13.

7. John Paul II, *Letter to the Elderly,* 9.

8. John Paul II, *Letter to the Elderly,* 7.

9. John Paul II, *Letter to the Elderly,* 18.

Youth: Future of the Church and the World

Theme: The Church treasures her youth, and challenges them to seek the highest truth and the greatest happiness in Jesus Christ.

Opening prayer: Father, we thank you for the young people in our lives and for all the young people in our world. We ask you to give them the grace to grow in the love and knowledge of your Son, Jesus Christ, and to realize that he alone can satisfy the deepest longings of their hearts. Inspire us to help them behold his face in the Church. Father, let your Spirit make a home in their hearts and lead them on the path of eternal happiness.

ABOUT JOHN PAUL II

From the earliest days of his priesthood, Karol Wojtyla had a special place in his heart for young people. As a young priest in Niegowice, he was put in charge of religious education in five elementary schools in nearby villages. He not only helped the children with their studies, he also played sports with them and organized their theatrical performances. In the evenings, he gathered them around bonfires in song and in prayer. Some of his parishioners referred to him as the "eternal teenager," because he seemed to relive his teenage years whenever he was with young people.

When Karol Wojtyla became pope, he continued his ministry to youth by embracing the young people of the world in an unprecedented way. The seed was planted in 1983 with a small group of teenagers who regularly met for prayer and fellowship at the Church of San Lorenzo near St. Peter's Square in Rome. Here, during one of these meetings, the idea of a worldwide gathering of youth was born as a way to bring together young Catholics from around the world for prayer and fellowship. When John Paul II was presented with the idea, he immediately gave it his blessing and full support.

The following year, during Palm Sunday weekend, more than three hundred thousand young people from all over the world accepted the pope's invitation to come to Rome for an international Jubilee on Youth. On the eve of Palm Sunday 1984, the pope called out to the crowd, "What a fantastic spectacle is presented on this stage by your gathering here today! Who claimed that today's youth has lost their sense of values? Is it really true that they cannot be counted on?"[1] On that day, John Paul II entrusted to the world's young people a symbol: a colossal wooden crucifix, later to be known as the World Youth Day Cross.

The success of this event prompted John Paul II to plan a similar gathering for the next year, and so in 1985, coinciding with the United Nations International Year of the Youth, 250,000 young people converged in Rome to be with the pope on Palm Sunday. On March 3, just prior to that event, John Paul II issued his *Letter to the World's Youth,* which focused on the responsibility that each generation bears for the future. The first official World Youth Day was celebrated in Rome in 1986. It was then repeated in 1987, after which World Youth Days were held every two years at various locations around the globe, with smaller, local versions on the alternate years.

John Paul II never missed a World Youth Day appointment, even when illness and frailty made it difficult for him to attend. He met the youth in Buenos Aires in 1987; Santiago de Compostela in 1989; Czestochowa, Poland, in 1991; Denver in 1993; Manila in 1995; Paris in 1997; Rome, during the Church's jubilee celebrations in 2000; and Toronto in 2002. These World Youth Day celebrations were attended by crowds numbering anywhere from half a million to a staggering seven million. The largest of these, held in Manila, is considered the largest gathering in human history.[2]

For those who attended a World Youth Day, the experience was transforming. Many left the conference feeling that their lives had been dramatically changed. Dominika Boczula, a pilgrim from Calgary, Canada, wrote, "I still feel something special inside of me every time I think about those amazing meetings with millions of people and one amazing, outstanding individual. No rock star, concert, or event can compare to the sheer multitudes and meaning which World Youth Day brings. I can't begin to imagine how many lives they have not only touched, but saved."[3]

Pause: How is it that John Paul II was able attract so many young people to Christ?

JOHN PAUL II's WORDS

Dear young people, many and enticing are the voices that call out to you from all sides: many of these voices speak to you of a joy that can be had with money, with success, with power. Mostly they propose a joy that comes with the superficial and fleeting pleasure of the senses.[4]

Dear friends, the aged pope, full of years but still young at heart, answers your youthful desire for happiness with words that are not his own. They are words that rang out two thousand years ago. Words that we have heard again tonight: "Blessed are they. . . ." The key word in Jesus' teaching is a proclamation of joy: "Blessed are they. . . ." People are made for happiness. Rightly, then, you thirst for happiness. Christ has the answer to this desire of yours. But he asks you to trust him. True joy is a victory, something which cannot be obtained without a long and difficult struggle. Christ holds the secret of this victory.[5]

What struggle are we talking about? Christ himself gives us the answer. "Though he was in the form of God," Saint Paul has written, he "did not count equality with God something to be grasped, but emptied himself, taking the form of a servant . . . he humbled himself and became obedient unto death" (Philippians 2:6-8). It was a struggle unto death. Christ fought this battle not for himself but for us. From his death, life has sprung forth. The tomb at Calvary has become the cradle of the new humanity on its journey to true happiness. The "Sermon on the Mount" marks out the map of this journey. The eight Beatitudes are the road signs that show the way. It is an uphill path, but he has walked it before us. He said one day: "He who follows me will not walk in darkness" (John 8:12). And at another time he added: "These things I have spoken to you, that my joy may be in you, and that your joy may be full" (John 15:11). It is by walking with Christ that we can achieve joy, true joy![6]

The joy promised by the Beatitudes is the very joy of Jesus himself: a joy sought and found in obedience to the Father and in the gift of self to others. . . . To believe in Jesus is to accept what he says, even when it runs contrary to what others are saying. It means rejecting the lure of sin, however attractive it may be.[7]

Young people listening to me, answer the Lord with strong and generous hearts! He is counting on you. Never forget: Christ needs you to carry out his plan of salvation! Christ needs your youth and your generous enthusiasm to make his proclamation of joy resound in the new millennium. Answer his call by placing your lives at his service in your brothers and sisters! Trust Christ, because He trusts you.[8]

REFLECTION

No single person touched the lives of so many young people and set their hearts on fire for Christ as Pope John Paul II did. During his papacy, he spoke to more than fourteen million youth and other pilgrims at ten international World Youth Days. John Paul II's message to the youth of the world was simple and cut straight to the heart: reject the lure of worldly pursuits, which lead only to fleeting superficial happiness, and reach instead for the true and lasting joy that comes from walking with and modeling one's life on Christ.

John Paul II did not downplay the sacrifice required to follow Christ. Like the rich young man in Mark's gospel who approached Jesus with the question, "Teacher, what must I do to inherit eternal life?" (Mark 10:17), we too are often torn between the desire for the deeper, truer joys of eternal life and the fleeting attractions of this world. These attachments caused the young man in the gospel account to walk away sad and unfulfilled. Yet, as John Paul II pointed out, we do not walk alone in this struggle, for our Lord is always there, beckoning and supporting: "He who follows me will not walk in darkness" (John 8:12).

Perhaps the reason why John Paul II was so effective in stirring the minds and hearts of the young is that he himself so completely and unhesitatingly followed Christ's call. He truly lived what he preached. Throughout his life, despite the fact that he suffered greatly, he never swerved from the mission given to him, and he truly loved those he served. Young people sensed his authenticity, and they responded with strong and generous hearts.

Questions for personal reflection and faith sharing:

❧ How can I, like John Paul II, treasure and nurture the young people in my life? How can I help them to know and seek the one thing that will bring them true and lasting happiness?

❧ As I think back to the days when I was a teenager, what was most important to me? Was there anyone who inspired me to follow Christ? If so, what was it about that person that affected me?

❧ Do I know people who have been to a World Youth Day gathering or encountered John Paul II at another gathering? What was their experience? What impact did it have on their life?

Guidance for prayer and action:

❧ What question would you ask Jesus if you were given the opportunity to speak with him in the flesh? Would you ask the same question as the young man in Mark's gospel? Ask yourself, "Do I have my priorities straight? Am I chasing after things that do not bring lasting joy? Am I obedient to what is true and good and whole in life? Do I have earthly treasures and attachments that keep me from giving my all to Christ and living my true dignity as a human being made in the image of God?"

🙏 In prayer, ask Jesus to send the Holy Spirit to give you the strength to keep your focus on him and to always do the will of God. Tell him of the earthly treasures and other attachments that you find difficult to give up, and ask his help in letting go of these things.

🙏 Read the Beatitudes (Matthew 5:1-12) and reflect upon their meaning for your life.

🙏 Consider going to the next World Youth Day gathering or other Catholic youth conferences that may be held regionally.

🙏 As an adult, get involved in youth ministry. Participate in intergenerational gatherings like a Catholic family conference, family retreats, or campouts that provide special opportunities for spiritual dialogue with young people. Pray that the young will experience the Church as their spiritual family. Instill in them the fact that they are the future of the Church, and assist them in their efforts to be on the forefront of evangelization.

🙏 Give the young people in your life plenty of role models in the saints. Focus on saints who made a great difference, even in their youth—saints like Catherine of Siena, Joan of Arc, Bernadette Soubirous, Thérèse of Lisieux, Agnes, Dominic Savio, among others. Share books and movies about the saints with them.

GOD'S WORD

For I know the plans I have for you, says the LORD, plans for welfare and not for evil, to give you a future and a hope.

—Jeremiah 29:11

Closing prayer: "Lord Jesus Christ, proclaim once more your Beatitudes in the presence of these young people. . . . Look upon them with love and listen to their young hearts, ready to put their future on the line for you. You have called them to be the 'salt of the earth and light of the world.' Continue to teach them the truth and beauty of the vision that you proclaimed on the Mountain. Make them men and women of the Beatitudes! Let the light of your wisdom shine upon them, so that in word and deed they may spread in the world the light and salt of the Gospel. Make their whole life a bright reflection of you, who are the true light that came into this world so that whoever believes in you will not die, but will have eternal life (John 3:16)!"[9]

1. "History of World Youth Day," www.wyd.ie/history.html.
2. Weigel, *Witness to Hope*, p. 750.
3. Dominika Boczula, "I Took the Pope's Word to Heart," *Western Catholic Reporter,* September 9, 2002.
4. John Paul II, 17th World Youth Day Papal Welcoming Ceremony Address, Toronto, July 25, 2002, 1.
5. 17th World Youth Day Address, 2.

6. 17th World Youth Day Address, 3.

7. 17th World Youth Day Address, 4.

8. 17th World Youth Day Address, 7, 4.

9. 17th World Youth Day Address, 8.

MEDITATION NINE
The Gifts of Marriage and Sexuality

Theme: Sacramental grace enables us to live God's love for us in marriage and to realize the deepest meaning of human sexuality.

Opening prayer: Father in heaven, we thank you for creating us in love, male and female. Thank you for the Sacrament of Matrimony and for drawing us to you in an eternal union of love and self-giving. As we ponder your design for marriage and sexuality as a path of holiness, we ask you to send your Holy Spirit to help us see your own image in ourselves, body and soul.

ABOUT JOHN PAUL II

In September 1979, less than a year after his election to the papacy, John Paul II began to unfold a profound new understanding of the human body and marital love. He called this first major teaching project of his papacy the Theology of the Body. It was developed in 129 short talks over the course of five years. Arising out of a clearly perceived need for a deeper perspective on the human body and human sexuality, the Theology of the Body answered the challenge posed to the Church by the sexual revolution and the backlash of bitter protest and discontent that had surfaced following the issuance of the encyclical *Humanae Vitae* by Pope Paul VI in 1968.

John Paul II's biographer, George Weigel, called the pope's Theology of the Body a "theological time bomb set to go off with dramatic consequences."[1] It has already shown signs of radically shifting the prevalent world view of love, sex, and marriage. By the third decade of John Paul II's pontificate, the Theology of the Body had spawned university courses, seminars, and study groups worldwide. Increasingly, a growing number of people have been seeking to explore the profound interconnections between sex and the deepest questions of human existence.

John Paul II's insights into the ultimate meaning of love, sex, and marriage were largely the fruit of many decades of pastoral work in Poland. In the early years of his priesthood, Father Wojtyla spent a great deal of time ministering to young adults and married couples—organizing and leading retreats, outings, catechesis, prayer meetings, and courses for engaged couples. He also encountered those in the confessional, as they spoke from the depths of their humanity. Over time, these two facets of his pastoral work afforded Father Wojtyla profound wisdom about the needs and concerns of married couples.

At the same time, major assaults on traditional Catholic sexual morality were sweeping through Poland and the West. The sexual revolution was coming into full swing, increasingly permissive abortion laws were being passed, and artificial methods of contraception were becoming more accessible. As a result, many people viewed sexuality as separate from both marriage and procreation. Losing sight of the moral value and purpose of sexuality led many to view children as problems to be solved rather than as gifts to be cherished.

Responding to these trends and conditions, Father Wojtyla produced his first written works dealing with human sexuality in 1960. *The Jeweler's Shop* was a meditation in the form of a play, in which he explored the mystery, the joys and pains, and the challenges of love and marriage. He also wrote *Love and Responsibility*, an in-depth philosophical treatment of the issues he had explored dramatically in *The Jeweler's Shop*. These two works became the basis of his Theology of the Body, which draws from Scripture to illustrate the divine purpose of human love and sexuality as a foreshadowing and a proclamation of the eternal union of Christ and the Church.

Pause: How can my vocation to marriage, the single life, or the religious life lead me to a deeper union with Christ?

JOHN PAUL II'S WORDS

Responsible parenthood is the necessary condition for human love, and it is also the necessary condition for authentic conjugal love, because love cannot be irresponsible. Its beauty is the fruit of responsibility. When love is truly responsible, it is also truly free.[2]

Love for a person excludes the possibility of treating him as an object of pleasure. . . . [But] the commandment of love is not limited to excluding all behavior that reduces the person to a mere object of pleasure. It requires more; it requires the affirmation of the person as a person. . . . Man, who is the only creature on earth that God wanted for his own sake, can fully discover himself only by the sincere giving of himself.[3]

Man affirms himself most completely by giving of himself. This is the fulfillment of the commandment of love. This is also the full truth about man, a truth that Christ taught us by His life, and that the tradition of Christian morality, no less than the tradition of saints and of the many heroes of love of neighbor, took up and lived out in the course of history. If we deprive human freedom of this possibility, if man does not commit himself to becoming a gift for others, then this freedom can become dangerous. It will become freedom to do what I myself consider as good, what brings me a profit or pleasure, even a sublimated pleasure. If we cannot accept the prospect of giving ourselves as a gift, then the danger of a selfish freedom will always be present.[4]

Dear married couples! Dear parents! . . . Sacramental grace—first in Baptism and Confirmation, then later in Matrimony—[pours] a fresh and powerful wave of supernatural love into your hearts. It is love which flows from the inner depths of the Blessed Trinity, of which the human family is an eloquent and living image. . . . This is a supernatural reality which helps you to sanctify your joys, to face hardships and sufferings, and to triumph over difficulties and moments of fatigue. In a word, it is a source of sanctification for you, and a source of strength for self-giving. It grows by constant prayer and above all by your sharing in the Sacraments of Reconciliation and of the Eucharist.[5]

REFLECTION

Many of us carry some amount of baggage of confused notions about the meaning and purpose of love, sex, and marriage. This is understandable, considering the conflicting messages we receive from the mass media, advertising, our schools, our peer groups, and our surroundings. There is no doubt that, at least on a sub-conscious level, these views influence the manner in which we approach our relationships with the opposite sex and, ultimately, marriage.

These messages tell us that love without commitment, sex outside of marriage, and sex as an end in itself are just as valid, if not better, options than the Christian view of marriage and sexuality. It is no wonder, then, that many of us who were not well grounded in the teachings of our faith took a different road. John Paul II was acutely aware that the children of the sexual revolution had to hear God's plan for marriage and sexuality in a fresh way, with unprecedented breadth and depth.

At the heart of John Paul II's persistent plea for us to live the gift of marriage and sexuality is the reality of true love itself—the total giving of one's self, as God has given himself to us in the person of Jesus Christ. Although total self-giving is not easy and can sometimes seem impossible, the grace that comes to us through the sacraments allows us to love beyond our expectations. With his grace, we are able regard ourselves and each other—mind, body, and soul—as nothing less than the embodiment of God's love.

Questions for personal reflection and faith sharing:

❧ If you are married: How have the sacraments helped me to live the Christian ideal of faithfulness and self-giving in my marriage? (Especially consider the Eucharist, matrimony, and reconciliation.) If you are not married: How does the sacramental life help me to live out my current calling to celibacy? How does it help me to view the possibility of marriage in the future? If you're a religious: How do the sacraments help me to live my vocation in true self-giving to those I serve?

❧ How can I more fully live out my marriage/single blessedness as a path of union with God?

❧ How can John Paul II's Theology of the Body deepen or challenge my understanding of Church teachings on nuptial love and sexuality?

Guidance for prayer and action:

❧ In an examination of conscience, ask the Holy Spirit to show you the state of your marriage as God sees it. You and your spouse can together ask yourselves: "Is God truly at the center of our marriage? Have we loved each other as God loves us? Are we faithful to each other in thought, word, and deed as God is ever-faithful to us? Have we been open to new life? Are we doing our very best to be God's presence to each other from day to day, from moment to moment? Are we doing our best to help each other get to heaven, so that together we may be united with God forever?" End your reflection with the Lord's Prayer.

๛ Meditate on the following Scripture passage, which expresses the nuptial dimension of the love that binds you to God: "I will betroth you to me for ever; I will betroth you to me in righteousness and in justice, in steadfast love, and in mercy. I will betroth you to me in faithfulness; and you shall know the LORD" (Hosea 2:19-20).

๛ If you do not already do so, establish a routine of praying daily with your spouse (and other family members). Set up an altar in a quiet place in your home. Light a candle, and make it a special time. Thank God for all your blessings, open up your private needs and concerns, and bring your petitions before God in prayer.

๛ In journaling, reflect upon the saving power of the sacraments, especially during a time of trial in your marriage. Write down how God poured a fresh and powerful wave of supernatural love into your heart through the sacraments. Consider passing on this story to loved ones as part of your spiritual legacy.

❧ Read John Paul II's Theology of the Body, along with commentaries that approach this profoundly scholarly work in laymen's language.[6] Participate in or start a Theology of the Body study group or attend a Theology of the Body seminar.

❧ Study the lives of married saints. Some recommended books: *Marriage as a Path to Holiness: Lives of Married Saints* by David Ford and Mary Ford; *Married Saints and Blesseds through the Centuries* by Ferdinand Holbock; and *Married Saints* by John F. Fink.

❧ Participate in an Engaged Encounter, Marriage Encounter Weekend, or Retrouvaille (for troubled marriages), which help couples to discover God's vision of marriage and family life, thereby leading them to a clearer understanding of their relationship with each other and with God. Learn about other ministries that the Church offers to married couples—including classes in Natural Family Planning—by calling the marriage and family life office of your diocese.

GOD'S WORD

Be subject to one another out of reverence for Christ. Wives, be subject to your husbands, as to the Lord. . . . Husbands, love your wives, as Christ loved the church and gave himself up for her. . . . "For this reason a man shall leave his father and mother and be joined to his wife, and the two shall become one flesh." This is a great mystery . . . in reference to Christ and the church.

—Ephesians 5:21-22, 25, 31-32

Closing prayer: "Lord, God of grace, you so love your people that you have carved us into the palm of your hand and through Christ and the Church you enrich us and strengthen us as your holy people. Look with favor on all who have committed themselves to one another in the sacrament of marriage. May they know your presence in good times and in bad, and willingly share with one another and with you the joys and struggles of their lives. May they never allow the sun to set on their anger but make them a clearer sign of the love of Christ for all people. Look with special favor on all those who are recently married and those who are preparing for marriage. Strengthen them, that all may see your love flowing from them. Bless those who struggle to maintain the bonds of love between them. May all married couples be for their families and friends, and for all the world, the sacrament of Christ's love for his bride, the Church. We ask this through Christ, our Lord. Amen."[7]

1. Weigel, *Witness to Hope*, p. 343.
2. John Paul II, *Crossing the Threshold of Hope*, p. 208.
3. John Paul II, *Crossing the Threshold of Hope*,
   pp. 200–202.
4. John Paul II, *Crossing the Threshold of Hope*, pp. 202–203.

5. John Paul II, Address at the World Meeting of Families, October 8, 1994, 6.
6. John Paul II, *Theology of the Body: Human Love in the Divine Plan* (Boston: Pauline Books and Media, 1997). For a list of commentaries see Resources on the Theology of the Body and Catholic Sexual Ethics, on p. 173.
7. Knights of Columbus Prayer for Married Couples.

MEDITATION TEN
The Domestic Church

Theme: Our mission to evangelize begins in the family, the domestic Church.

Opening prayer: Father, we thank you for all the members of our family, who make it possible for us to live out your love for us in our joys as well as our sorrows. Help us to always regard our family as our primary path to you, and guide us in the ways that you call us to be Church in our own homes. Grant us the grace to always be a reflection of the love that your heavenly family shares.

ABOUT JOHN PAUL II

As a child Karol Wojtyla, nicknamed Lolek, was raised in a home that was, at the same time, Church—the universal Church in miniature. From his parents, the elder Karol and Emilia, Lolek learned his first prayers and heard his first verses of Scripture. The first altar he knelt at was one his parents had arranged in the parlor of their modest apartment in Wadowice. Located across the street from St. Mary's Church, the Wojtylas' home was arranged to serve as a domestic Church with its well-used altar, religious art on the walls, and font of holy water by the door.

When Lolek was nine years old, his mother died of heart and kidney failure, leaving him and his father virtually alone. His only brother, Edmund, was away at school, and would die a few years later from scarlet fever while practicing as a young doctor. His only sister, Olga, had died in infancy. At the death of his wife, Karol senior, who had already retired with the rank of captain in the Polish army, focused his attention on Lolek. A self-taught man who was fluent in several languages, he aided in his son's education, teaching him German, history, poetry, and literature.

Karol senior was deeply involved in Lolek's religious formation. Together, they attended Mass at St. Mary's Church, where Lolek served as an altar boy. They read the Bible and prayed the rosary regularly. They often went on pilgrimages to Kalwaria Zebrzydowska, a great outdoor shrine whose annual passion play on the feast of the Assumption drew millions of Catholics from all over Poland.

In his autobiographical recollections, John Paul II remembers his father as "a man of constant prayer." He would often find him on his knees, in silent prayer. His father's example was, in a way, "my first seminary," writes John Paul II, "a kind of domestic seminary."[1] In addition to teaching him the rudiments of the faith, the elder Karol instilled in Lolek the mystery of the Church, with its "invisible dimension" that is larger than the visible structure and organization of the Church.[2] He also taught him, by example and admonition, that the life of faith begins with interior conversion. Karol senior died of a heart attack in the winter of 1941. By the age of twenty-one, Karol had lost all his family.

Decades later, in 1978, Karol Wojtyla became "papa" to his universal family of more than a billion souls. In his care of this family, Pope John Paul II often took time during his pastoral travels to listen to the concerns of families. He canonized a number of married couples, and devoted two of his major writings to the family: *Familiaris Consortio* (The Family in the Modern World), and his *Letter to Families*. He also treated various aspects of family life in his encyclical *Evangelium Vitae* (The Gospel of Life), in his apostolic letter *Mulieris Dignitatem* (The Dignity of Women), and in his Theology of the Body, which delves into God's design for marriage and human sexuality. He established the Pontifical Council for the Family, which helps Christian families fulfill their educational and apostolic mission through various ministries in the Church. He also established the Pontifical Institute for Studies on Marriage and Family, with campuses in various parts of the world. The institute helps to prepare a new generation of leaders and servants of marriage and the family through the study of philosophy, theology, social science, and pastoral care.

Pause: What is it about Karol Wojtyla's family life or John Paul II's ministry to the family that I find most inspiring?

JOHN PAUL II'S WORDS

Dear Christian families, . . . the Church built on the foundation of the Apostles begins with you: "*Ecclesiola*—domestic Church."[3]

The Christian family, as the "domestic Church," forms the original and fundamental school for training in the faith. The father and mother receive, in the Sacrament of

Matrimony, the grace and the responsibility of providing Christian education for their children, to whom they bear witness and transmit, at one and the same time, human and religious values. To be instruments of the heavenly Father in the work of forming their own children—here is found the inviolable limit that parents must respect in carrying out their mission. They must never consider themselves "owners" of their children, but rather they must educate them, paying constant attention to the privileged relationship that their children have with their Father in heaven. In the last analysis, as with Jesus, it is his business that they must "be about" (Luke 2:49).[4]

Catholic parents must learn to form their family as a "domestic Church," a church in the home as it were, where God is honored, his law is respected, prayer is a normal event, virtue is transmitted by word and example, and everyone shares the hopes, the problems and sufferings of everyone else.[5]

Through God's mysterious design, it was in that family that the Son of God spent long years of a hidden life. It is therefore the prototype and example for all Christian families. . . . It underwent trials of poverty, persecution and exile. It glorified God in an incomparably exalted and pure way. And it will not fail to help Christian families—indeed, all the families in the world—to be faithful to their day-to-day duties, to bear the cares and tribulations of life, to be open and generous to the needs of others, and to fulfill with joy the plan of God in their regard.[6]

REFLECTION

In striving to remain committed to the faith in an atmosphere of widespread unbelief, invasive secularism, and radical individualism, Christian families face an uphill battle. Fortunately, we are not alone. We can rely on the grace that has enabled Christian families throughout the ages to pass on the faith to succeeding generations—our sharing in God's own life. This is the very life we're called to live in the domestic church, a life as earthly as it is heavenly.

Along with the frustrations, the sorrows, and the fatigue that come with family life, we also know that we can count on the first and eternal family—Father, Son, and Holy Spirit—as our unfailing source of joy and strength. The Holy Trinity, as well as the Holy Family—Jesus, Mary, and Joseph, the earthly manifestation of this communion—are not merely ideals of what family life should be. They are, in fact, our family, in the same sense that the Church is also our family: a family whose destiny is to live out and proclaim God's love for all; a family that death cannot separate; a family whose true home is heaven. When *this reality is rooted in the heart* of Christian families, John Paul II said that it cannot—and should not—remain a family secret. In drawing its life from Jesus Christ, every family's daily life not only takes on extraordinary meaning and purpose, it also becomes its most fundamental, and overflowing, witness to the faith. Such a life can only find great joy in spreading the good news.[7]

Questions for personal reflection and faith sharing:

🌾 How did my family live its life as a domestic Church when I was a child? How did we pray together and extend God's love to others? What family traditions did we have that helped me to grow in my faith?

🌾 What is the biggest challenge that my family faces in its day-to-day life as a domestic Church? What can we do to overcome this challenge?

🌾 What can I do to help my family more deeply live its calling to be a domestic Church—to live and proclaim God's love in all aspects of daily life?

Guidance for prayer and action:

🌾 In an examination of conscience, ask yourself: Is my family life centered around the "Father's business"? Are we living a life of communion sustained and driven by love? Do we serve life, by being responsibly open to new life through procreation? Are we passionate about handing on the fruits of the moral, spiritual, and supernatural life to and through our children? Do we share in the life and mission of the Church? Do we participate in the development of society? Pray for the Holy Spirit to guide your family to fulfill its calling to be an intimate community of life and love, and to live out its mission to make God's love known to everyone it encounters.

❧ Make time each day to gather your family in prayer. John Paul II highlighted the rosary as a prayer of and for the family. He noted that when individual family members turn their eyes to Jesus while praying the rosary, they also regain the ability to look one another in the eye, to communicate, to show solidarity, to forgive one another, and to see their covenant of love renewed in the Spirit of God.[8]

❧ Develop the habit of reading the Scriptures together as a family. It also helps to read the gospel for the following Sunday to prepare for Mass, and to think about how the gospel applies to situations that arise during the week.

❧ Arrange your home in a way that communicates the truth, beauty, and richness of your faith. Make a family altar with a prominent spot for your family Bible. Hang crucifixes in as many places as you can, and display pictures and paintings of the Holy Family, the saints, and other role models in the faith.

❧ Make family pilgrimages to Catholic shrines, abbeys, and historical sites. You can find a list of Catholic shrines in the United States at catholicshrines.net and in *Catholic Shrines and Places of Pilgrimage in the United States* (Washington, DC: National Conference of Catholic Bishops, 1998) and *The Lig-*

uori Guide to Catholic USA: A Treasury of Churches, Schools, Monuments, Shrines, and Monasteries (Missouri: Liguori Publications, 1999).

✦ Make use of the Catholic mass media to keep learning about your faith as a family and to keep abreast of issues of importance to the Church. Subscribe to your diocesan newspaper and other Catholic publications, and tune in to Catholic television and radio stations. (See pp. 174–175 for a list of Catholic media resources.)

✦ Keep a scrapbook of how your family grows in the faith. Be creative and colorful in putting together memorabilia that tell how you live, celebrate, and observe your Christian faith in its depth, beauty, and richness. Write down vignettes of memorable experiences—your joys as well as your sorrows—in which your faith sustained you. Pass this on as a spiritual legacy to your family.

✦ If your family is suffering from separation, divorce, or other crises, take advantage of the various ministries offered by the Church. Contact your parish office or the marriage and family life office of your diocese for these resources. Reach out to other families for aid and comfort. Ask others to pray with and for you.

✦ Consecrate your family to Jesus. You can do this by gathering your family together and saying a special prayer that acknowledges Jesus as Lord and dedicates the life of your family to his service. Or, you can utilize the Apostolate for Family Consecration, which has the blessing of Pope John Paul II and instructs families in the act of consecration. (For more information, visit www.familyland.org and click on Family Consecration.)

❧ Read the lives of holy families in the Church, such as Sts. Nona and Gregory and their offspring, Sts. Gregory, Gorgonia, and Caesarius; Sts. Basil the Elder and Emmelia, whose offspring include Saints Macrina the Younger, Gregory of Nyssa, and Basil the Great; Blesseds Luigi Beltrame Quattrocchi and Maria Corsini and family; and Venerable Louis and Zelie Martin and family, which includes St. Thérèse of Lisieux.

❧ Evangelize other families. One of the best ways to reach out to other families is to invite them to your home. Share the love, the food, and the joy of your faith in these gatherings. Share ideas on how your family can spread the great blessings of the Catholic faith with other families.

GOD'S WORD

After three days they found him in the temple, sitting among the teachers, listening to them and asking them questions; and all who heard him were amazed at his understanding and his answers. And when they saw him they were astonished; and his mother said to him, "Son, why have you treated us so? Behold, your father and I have been looking for you anxiously." And he said to them, "How is it that you sought me? Did you not know that I must be in my Father's house?" And they did not understand the saying which he spoke to them. And he went down with them and came to Nazareth, and was obedient to them; and his mother kept all these things in her heart.

And Jesus increased in wisdom and in stature, and in favor with God and man.

—Luke 2:46-52

Closing prayer: "Lord God, from you every family in heaven and on earth takes its name. Father, you are Love and Life. Through your Son, Jesus Christ, born of woman, and through the Holy Spirit, fountain of divine charity, grant that every family on earth may become for each successive generation a true shrine of life and love. Grant that your grace may guide the thoughts and actions of husbands and wives for the good of their families and of all the families in the world. Grant that the young may find in the family solid support for their human dignity and for their growth in truth and love. Grant that love, strengthened by the grace of the sacrament of marriage, may prove mightier than all the weakness and trials through which our families sometimes pass. Through the intercession of the Holy Family of Nazareth, grant that the Church may fruitfully carry out her worldwide mission in the family and through the family. Through Christ our Lord, who is the Way, the Truth, and the Life for ever and ever. Amen."[9]

1. John Paul II, *Gift and Mystery* (New York: Doubleday, 1996), p. 20.
2. John Paul II, *Crossing the Threshold of Hope,* p. 142.
3. John Paul II, Homily, Eucharistic Celebration on the Occasion of the World Meeting with Families, October 9, 1994, 5.
4. John Paul II, Homily, Prato, Italy, March 19, 1986, 4.
5. John Paul II, Homily at Aqueduct Racetrack, October 6, 1995, 7.
6. John Paul II, Apostolic Exhortation *Familiaris Consortio* (The Family in the Modern World), November 22, 1981, 86.
7. John Paul II, *Familiaris Consortio,* 52.
8. John Paul II, *Rosarium Virginis Mariae,* 41.
9. John Paul II, Prayer for the Family, Themes for Reflection and Dialogue for the Fourth World Meeting of the Family, January 25–26, 2003.

MEDITATION ELEVEN

Penance, Forgiveness, and Reconciliation

Theme: Penance is a conversion that passes from the heart to deeds, and then to the Christian's whole life.

Opening prayer: Father in heaven, we thank you for your infinite mercy and for giving us your Son, through whom you have reconciled us to yourself. Send your Holy Spirit to search our hearts and to help us see clearly how we stand before you. Lead us on the path of sincere penance and full reconciliation with you and with all those we have wronged. Through our new life in Christ, may we fulfill our calling to help reconcile all people to you and to one another.

ABOUT JOHN PAUL II

In a taped message given shortly after the assassination attempt on John Paul II's life in 1981, the Holy Father said, "I pray for that brother of ours who shot me, and whom I have sincerely pardoned."[1] Two years later, on December 27, 1983, John Paul II celebrated Mass at Rebibbia Prison and visited his attacker, Mehmet Ali Agca, in his cell. During the meeting, the pope embraced Agca, who in turn kissed the pontiff's hand. Most of their twenty-minute conversation was private, but the encounter between John Paul II and Mehmet Ali Agca left a deep impression upon the millions who witnessed it in the media. It exemplified John Paul II's deep commitment to the principle of forgiveness and reconciliation as an essential element of any effort toward peace.

Although the attempt on his life caused him grave injuries, John Paul II saw in it an opportunity for the Church to reflect upon the roots of conflict and division, both in its personal and social dimensions. A few years later, John Paul II led the Church into an examination of the Christian response to discord, wherever it exists. In his 1984 apostolic exhortation *Reconciliatio et Paenitentia* (Reconciliation and Penance), he called upon all members of the Church to continually strive to be in full reconciliation with God and with one another.

In preparation for the Great Jubilee celebration, John Paul II wrote in his 1994 apostolic letter *On the Coming of the Third Millennium* that while the Great Jubilee of the year 2000 would be a time of joyful celebration, the joy should be based on forgiveness and reconciliation. Four years later, in a formal proclamation of the Great Jubilee, *Mystery of the Incarnation of the Son of God*, John Paul II wrote, "As the Successor of Peter, I ask that in this year of mercy the Church, strong in the holiness which she receives from her Lord, should kneel before God and implore forgiveness for the past and present sins of her sons and daughters."[2]

It was the first time in the entire history of the Church that a pope had made such a request. In none of the previous jubilees had there been an awareness of any faults in the Church's past or of the need to ask God's pardon for the Church's conduct.

Against the advice of some cardinals opposed to the enormous complexity of digging through two thousand years of history, the pope appointed a team of scholars to catalog the Church's misdeeds in order to lay a factual foundation for self-examination. At his request, in 1999 the International Theological Commission issued *Memory and Reconciliation: The Church and the Faults of the Past*, which reflects upon the biblical and theological foundations of the pope's request for a public confession of the Church's past sins and the hope such a confession offers for the present and future life of the Church.

On the first Sunday of Lent in 2000, John Paul II led the Church in a public confession of past and present sins with a Mass of reconciliation and a ceremony for a "purification of memory." On behalf of the Church, John Paul II confessed sins committed in the service of truth and sins committed against Jews, women, indigenous peoples, the unborn, and other groups.[3] Turning to present-day failures, John Paul II asked Catholics to consider how much they had allowed themselves to be influenced by the prevailing climate of secularism and ethical relativism.

Pause: How does John Paul II's example challenge me to pursue a more deeply penitential life and to be fully reconciled to God and to all people?

John Paul II's Words

The term and the very concept of penance are very complex. If we link penance with the metanoia which the synoptics refer to, it means the inmost change of heart under the influence of the word of God and in the perspective of the kingdom. But penance also means changing one's life in harmony with the change of heart, and in this sense doing penance is completed by bringing forth fruits worthy of penance. It is one's whole existence that becomes penitential, that is to say, directed toward a continuous striving for what is better. But doing penance is something authentic and effective only if it is translated into deeds and acts of penance. In this sense penance means, in the Christian theological and spiritual vocabulary, asceticism, that is to say, the concrete daily effort of a person, supported by God's grace, to lose his or her own life for Christ as the only means of gaining it; an effort to put off the old man and put on the new; an effort to overcome in oneself what is of the flesh in order that what is spiritual may prevail; a continual effort to rise from the things of here below to the things of above, where Christ is. Penance is therefore a conversion that passes from the heart to deeds and then to the Christian's whole life.

In each of these meanings penance is closely connected with reconciliation, for reconciliation with God, with oneself, and with others implies overcoming that radical break which is sin. And this is achieved only through the interior transformation or conversion which bears fruit in a person's life through acts of penance. . . . Sacred Scripture speaks to us of this reconciliation, inviting us to make every effort to attain it (2 Corinthians 5:20). But Scripture also tells us that it is above all a merciful gift of God to humanity (Romans 5:11). The history of salvation—the salvation of the whole of humanity as well as of every human being of whatever period—is the wonderful history of a reconciliation: the reconciliation whereby God, as Father, in the blood and the cross of his Son made man, reconciles the world to himself and thus brings into being a new family of those who have been reconciled.[4]

REFLECTION

To forgive and to ask for forgiveness can sometimes be the most difficult—seemingly impossible—acts that our Lord asks of us (Matthew 18:21-22; 6:12). True forgiveness requires not simply gestures of civility but a continued state of being and doing. John Paul II's apostolic exhortation *Reconciliation and Penance* came at a time when the Church found itself grappling with a secular culture that does not encourage people to form their consciences or use them as a guide for right action. In commenting upon this prevailing crisis of conscience, John Paul II noted that contemporary men and women seem to find it harder than ever to recognize their own mistakes and seem very reluctant to say "I repent" or "I am sorry" or to make amends for their transgressions. Given this situation, consider what a stretch it was for many people to be asked to repent not only for sins they did not personally commit but that were committed centuries before they were born!

While John Paul II's personal act of forgiveness was greatly admired, his request to ask forgiveness for the Church's past sins was met with fears that a public confession would open old wounds, stir up bitterness, and shake the faith of many. Yet, to John Paul II, there were no shortcuts to reconciliation. Reconciling with God and with man meant confessing before God and man, with all the trouble and the risks it may entail, and doing everything possible to pave the path of restored relationships. Further, he challenged us to see the Church as one body, with her holy as well as unholy memories, in communion with both her saints and her sinners, from all generations. In asking forgiveness before those we have wronged, John Paul II requested that we do so "without seeking anything in return, but strengthened only by 'the love of God which has been poured into our hearts' (Romans 5:5)."[5]

Questions for personal reflection and faith sharing:

❦ What is God asking of me so that I may be fully reconciled with him and with all those I have wronged?

❦ What weaknesses do I need to overcome in my attempts to live a truly penitential life—to live penance as an ongoing and deepening conversion in Christ that permeates my whole life?

☙ How have I experienced the burden of the Church's past sins, in my own heart and in my encounters with those who have justly or unjustly accused it of certain wrongs? How may God be calling to me to restore relationships with those who feel alienated from the Church because of its past sins? How can I witness to the grace that has abounded in the Church, especially when sin also abounded? (see Romans 5:20).

Guidance for prayer and action:

☙ Receive the Sacrament of Reconciliation frequently. To prepare for a good confession with the intention of purifying your memory, think of the people you have wronged, as well as those who have wronged you, and the burden that the sins committed may still place on your heart. If possible, place yourself in the presence of our Lord Jesus Christ before the Holy Eucharist when you do this recollection. Pray, "Lord, I wish to be unburdened of sins that I have committed and that others have committed against me. Have mercy on us, Lord. Please grant me and all those concerned the grace of forgiveness and full reconciliation with you and with each other."

☙ Write a letter of confession to God, in which you revisit occasions when sin marred your relationship with him. Tell your loving and merciful Father everything you've done that you are deeply sorry for. If you are the wronged party, you may tell him about your difficulties in forgiving those who sinned against you. Ask the Holy Spirit to give you comfort and strength when painful memories resurface. Also ask the mother of our Lord to pray with you. Pray, "Lord Jesus, please take these painful memories and plunge them into your love, not to destroy them, but to cause them to give hope and to help me to do better. Please give me the grace to forgive without asking anything in return. Help me to create or make way for opportunities to make amends with all whom I have wronged. Let me die to sin and rise to new life in you." End with the Lord's Prayer.

✿ Help reconcile those in conflict. In your prayers, remember those who are experiencing conflict and division (such as those in troubled marriages, estranged family members and friends, groups divided by religious beliefs, tribes and nations at war, etc.). Ask the Holy Spirit to guide you in whatever steps you're called to take to help them be reconciled with God, with themselves, and with their neighbors. As John Paul II teaches, "The message of reconciliation has . . . been entrusted to the whole community of believers, to the whole fabric of the Church, that is to say, the task of doing everything possible to witness to reconciliation and to bring it about in the world."[6]

✿ Meditate on the Lord's words to the apostles in the Upper Room after his resurrection, "Peace be with you." After showing them the wounds on his hands and his side, he said, "As the Father has sent me, even so I send you. . . . Receive the Holy Spirit. If you forgive the sins of any, they are forgiven; if you retain the sins of any, they are retained" (John 20:21-23).

❧ Witness to the graces you have received through the Sacrament of Reconciliation to family and friends. Let them know how God "breathes" new life into you through this sacrament (see John 20:22).

❧ Practice forms of devotion to the Divine Mercy that our Lord entrusted to St. Faustina Kowalska: the veneration of the Image of the Divine Mercy; the feast of Mercy (Divine Mercy Sunday); the Chaplet; the Novena to the Divine Mercy; and prayer at 3 o'clock in the afternoon, the Hour of Great Mercy. The pope was deeply committed to these devotions and their propagation, and spoke about how they can help us "look with new eyes at our brothers and sisters, with an attitude of unselfishness and solidarity, of generosity and forgiveness."[7] Information on the history of these devotions and how to practice them is available at Catholic bookstores and on the Internet.

GOD'S WORD

Hide thy face from my sins,
    and blot out all my iniquities.
Create in me a clean heart, O God,
    and put a new and right spirit within me.
—Psalm 51:9, 10

Closing prayer: "Most merciful Father, your Son, Jesus Christ, the judge of the living and the dead, in the humility of his first coming redeemed humanity from sin and in his glorious return he will demand an account of every sin. Grant that our forebearers, our brothers and sisters, and we, your servants, who by the grace of the Holy Spirit turn back to you in wholehearted repentance, may experience your mercy and receive the forgiveness of our sins. We ask this through Christ our Lord. Amen."[8]

1. Weigel, *Witness to Hope,* p. 41.
2. John Paul II, Bull of Indiction of the Great Jubilee of the Year 2000 *Incarnationis Mysterium* (The Mystery of the Incarnation), November 29, 1998, 11.
3. John Paul II with representatives of the Roman Curia, *Universal Prayer: Confessions of Sins and Asking for Forgiveness,* March 12, 2000.
4. John Paul II, Apostolic Exhortation *Reconciliatio et Paenitentia* (Reconciliation and Penance), December 2, 1984, 4.
5. John Paul II, *Incarnationis Mysterium* 11.
6. John Paul II, *Reconciliatio et Paenitentia,* 8.
7. John Paul II, Homily, Mass for the Canonization of Sister Mary Faustina Kowalska, April 30, 2000, 5.
8. John Paul II, Concluding Prayer, *Universal Prayer: Confessions of Sins and Asking for Forgiveness,* March 12, 2000.

MEDITATION TWELVE
The Christian Meaning of Suffering

Theme: Christ reveals the meaning and value of our suffering.

Opening prayer: Father in heaven, help me to see my own suffering and the suffering of all humanity in the light of the life, passion, death, and resurrection of your beloved Son, Jesus. Grant me the grace to see the redeeming value of my suffering and to find peace in following you even in times of great trial.

ABOUT JOHN PAUL II

John Paul II was no stranger to suffering. Early in life he lost his mother, sister, brother, and father to untimely deaths. As an underground seminarian during World War II, he was wounded by a German truck in a hit-and-run accident. During the war, he lived in poverty and faced the constant threat of death while witnessing the unspeakable evils of the Nazi regime and suffering the loss of many dear friends. Following the war, he lived through the oppressive policies of the totalitarian communist regime.

John Paul II's health suffered its first major blow in 1981, when the assassination attempt on his life caused sustained injuries. The assassin's bullet shattered his colon and small intestine, causing him to lose three-fourths of his blood from internal hemorrhaging. Twenty-two inches of his intestines had to be cut away, the colon lacerations sewn up, and injuries to his right shoulder and a finger on his left hand (caused when the bullet exited his body) treated during a five-and-a-half-hour operation. After recovering from this incident, John Paul II wrote *Salvifici Doloris*, a deep and moving apostolic letter on the Christian meaning of suffering, issued on February 11, 1984.

In spite of those wounds, the pope was in good health until the early 1990s, when he began suffering from slurred speech and hearing difficulty. His physical condition worsened after a fall that broke his leg in 1994. After a hip replacement, he could no longer walk without difficulty. The ravages of Parkinson's disease then set in, a condition which was not officially confirmed until 2003. In February 2005, John Paul suffered from an inflammation of the larynx resulting from influenza. After a tracheotomy was performed, the pope's severely weakened condition gave rise to the various complications that led to his death on April 2, 2005.

As the world witnessed John Paul II's suffering, it became increasingly evident that the pope practiced what he taught. He bore his cross in a spirit of surrender to God's will, with eternity in sight. As he offered his sufferings for the welfare of the Church, he gave powerful testimony to the truth that "the good shepherd lays down his life for his sheep" (John 10:11).

Pause: How does John Paul II's attitude toward the trials in his life speak to me about my own suffering and the suffering of others?

JOHN PAUL II's WORDS

Down through the centuries and generations, it has been seen that in suffering there is concealed a particular power that draws a person interiorly close to Christ, a special grace. . . . This interior process does not always follow the same pattern. . . . But in general it can be said that almost always the individual enters suffering with a typically human protest and with the question "why." . . . He often puts this question to God, and to Christ. Furthermore, he cannot help noticing that the one to whom he puts the question is himself suffering and wishes to answer him from the Cross, from the heart of his own suffering. . . . The answer which comes through this sharing, by way of the interior encounter with the Master, is in itself something more than the mere abstract answer to the question about the meaning of suffering. . . . Christ does not explain in the abstract the reasons for suffering, but before all else he says: "Follow me!" Come!. . . . Gradually, as the individual takes up his cross, spiritually uniting himself to the Cross of Christ, the salvific meaning of suffering is revealed before him. He does not discover this meaning at his own human level, but at the level of the suffering of Christ. At the same time, however, from this level of Christ, the salvific meaning of suffering descends to man's level and becomes, in a sense, the individual's personal response. It is then that man finds in his suffering interior peace and even spiritual joy.[1]

Saint Paul speaks of such joy in the Letter to the Colossians: "I rejoice in my sufferings for your sake" (1:24). A source of joy is found in the overcoming of the sense of the uselessness of suffering, a feeling that is sometimes very strongly rooted in human suffering. . . . The discovery of the salvific meaning of suffering in union with Christ transforms this depressing feeling. Faith in sharing in the suffering of Christ brings with it the interior certainty that the suffering person "completes what is lacking in Christ's afflictions"; the certainty that in the spiritual dimension of the work of Redemption he is serving, like Christ, the salvation of his brothers and sisters. Therefore he is carrying out an irreplaceable service.[2]

In the messianic program of Christ . . . suffering is present in the world in order to release love, in order to give birth to works of love towards neighbor, in order to transform the whole of human civilization into a "civilization of love." . . . Christ said: "You did it to me." He himself is the one who in each individual experiences love . . . when this is given to every suffering person without exception. He himself is present in this suffering person. . . . At one and the same time, Christ has taught man to do good by his suffering and to do good to those who suffer. In this double aspect he has completely revealed the meaning of suffering.[3]

REFLECTION

Suffering touches us all. In the depths of the pain that suffering brings, whether it is physical, mental, emotional, or spiritual in nature, personal or collective, we can't help but ask, "Why?" "Why must I go through this?" "Why does God allow evil to bring unspeakable suffering in this world?"

John Paul II reassures us that when we pose such questions, we can trust that God not only hears us but responds with an ultimate act of love. We suffer whenever we experience any kind of evil.[4] God, in his infinite love for his creation, reaches into the very roots of evil—sin and death. By becoming man, God revealed himself as no mere observer of human suffering, but as a God who is sensitive to every human suffering, whether of the body or of the soul. He healed the sick, consoled the afflicted, and fed the hungry. He freed people from various physical disabilities, such as deafness, blindness, and leprosy. He freed them from the devil and restored the dead to life. In his passion and death on the cross, he emptied himself of all power in order to transcend human suffering so he could take upon himself the sufferings and the sins of all.[5] Through his resurrection, he gave us a glimpse of the glory hidden in our suffering as well as the strength to move forward through the thick of darkness.

Christ's life shows us that our own suffering can be transformed by God's love working in us. Through his suffering, Christ makes himself present in every human suffering and acts from within that suffering by the powers of his consoling Spirit. It is in closely uniting ourselves to him on the cross, as Mary did, that our suffering is given fresh life by the power of this cross and becomes "no longer the weakness of man but the power of God."[6]

Questions for personal reflection and faith sharing:

How have I felt God reaching deep into my heart through an experience of personal suffering? How has this experience changed me?

How have I been called to help bear someone else's cross? How have I grown through this experience?

How have I experienced the redeeming value of suffering when it's joined to Christ's suffering? How can I make use of this experience to glorify God and strengthen those who are suffering?

Guidance for prayer and action:

Draw strength to cope with suffering from the Eucharist. In receiving Christ in the Eucharist, we receive the life of the risen Christ (John 6:54)—"the spiritual power necessary to confront all obstacles and trials, and to remain faithful to our commitment as Christians."[7] Receive the Blessed Sacrament as frequently as possible, and offer all your sufferings to the Lord during the Eucharistic sacrifice. Draw close to Christ in prayer at eucharistic adoration. John Paul II relied on daily reception of the Eucharist and on eucharistic adoration for strength, consolation, and support in bearing his own sufferings.[8]

❧ Pray repeatedly, "Jesus, I trust in you." This is a prayer that the Lord asked St. Faustina to have inscribed on his image of Divine Mercy. It clearly expresses the attitude with which we too are called to abandon ourselves trustfully in the hands of the Lord in times of suffering.[9]

❧ Meditate upon or write about the crosses you are bearing, and pour your heart out to the Lord. Feel free to tell him exactly how you feel about the suffering you're going through. Ask him for the grace to unite your sufferings with his passion, to bear them in love for God and all else concerned, and to raise you up whenever you fall. Also remember to offer your sufferings for the salvation of those in need of help. End your meditation by praising and thanking God for all the blessings in your life, and by praying the Lord's Prayer.

❧ Unite your sufferings with Christ's passion and death by making the Stations of the Cross. Then ask Jesus to stay with you and to draw you to himself. Also ask him to stay with you through his mother, to whom, from the cross, he entrusted every human being (John 19:27).

❧ Pray for and with others who are suffering. Doing so teaches us that prayer illuminates the heart and opens the soul to understanding the pain of others.[10]

❧ Ask others to pray with you and for you. Do not hesitate to share your burdens with loved ones and to trust in the power of prayer to strengthen you.

❧ Ask the saints to be with you in times of suffering. You may call upon saints who in their lifetime experienced a form of suffering similar to yours. You may, for instance, call upon St. Monica for persistence in prayer when a loved one leaves the Church; St. Teresa of Avila, whose illnesses brought her closer to God; or any of the saints who cheerfully risked rejection, prison, torture, and death to proclaim the message of Jesus Christ.

❧ Help those who are suffering by showing them God's love in a concrete way. Send a card, make a phone call, or bring over a meal. Our sufferings are alleviated when we experience the love and comfort of our brothers and sisters.

GOD'S WORD

So we do not lose heart. Though our outer nature is wasting away, our inner nature is being renewed every day. For this slight momentary affliction is preparing for us an eternal weight of glory beyond all comparison, because we look not to the things that are seen but to the things that are unseen; for the things that are seen are transient, but the things that are unseen are eternal.

—2 Corinthians 4:16-18

Closing prayer: Lord Jesus, I bring before you in prayer all those I know and love and all people throughout the world who are suffering in body, mind, or spirit. Lord, help them to find strength in you, and give them relief from their burdens. Hear their prayers, O Lord, and let them know the peace that only you can give. Amen.

1. John Paul II, Apostolic Letter *Salvifici Doloris* (On the Christian Meaning of Human Suffering), February 11, 1984, 26.
2. John Paul II, *Salvifici Doloris,* 27.
3. John Paul II, *Salvifici Doloris,* 30.
4. John Paul II, *Salvifici Doloris,* 7.
5. John Paul II, *Salvifici Doloris,* 17.
6. John Paul II, *Salvifici Doloris,* 26.
7. John Paul II, General Audience, June 8, 1983, 3.
8. John Paul II, *Ecclesia de Eucharistia,* 25.
9. John Paul II, Homily, Divine Mercy Sunday, April 22, 2001, 6.
10. John Paul II, Address to the Secular Institute "Servants of Suffering," December 2, 2004, 3.

That We May All Be One

Theme: Prayer is the soul of ecumenism and of interreligious dialogue.

Prayer: Father, we pray that your Son's prayer for unity may fully penetrate our hearts and overcome everything that divides us. Give us the grace to look into the source of these divisions in our own hearts, and to root them out with your own love for us. May the example set by your servant, Pope John Paul II, help us to recognize and to live out the unity that already exists among all people, especially in the common prayer of those who desire to know and follow you.

ABOUT JOHN PAUL II

As a child, Karol Wojtyla grew up in a town that, although predominantly Catholic, had a Jewish population of more than 1,200, a synagogue, and a Jewish cemetery. A number of his childhood friends and playmates were Jews, some of whom remained lifelong friends. As pope, he reflected, "I can vividly remember the Jews who gathered every Saturday at the synagogue behind our school. Both religious groups, Catholics and Jews, were united, I presumed, by the awareness that they prayed to the same God."[1]

Karol Wojtyla's understanding of the Catholic Church's relationship to members of other Christian and non-Christian religions was profoundly deepened by his participation in the proceedings of the Second Vatican Council. The Council involved representatives from various Christian churches as well as non-Christian religions, who, together with Catholics, blazed a path of common prayer and dialogue. Little did Bishop Karol Wojtyla know that he would one day play a global role in helping this vision take root and flourish in the hearts of many followers of the world's religions.

In his efforts to help break down longstanding divisions among Christians and non-Christians, John Paul II became the first pope to enter a synagogue and a mosque and the first pope ever to preach in a Lutheran church. As the world saw John Paul II engaged in these historical interreligious encounters, it became apparent that he truly respected and appreciated the rays of truth found in other religions. He genuinely reflected the recognition given to other religious traditions by the Second Vatican Council in its decree on interreligious dialogue, *Nostra Aetate*.

One such encounter was the Holy Father's visit to the Umayyad Mosque in the heart of Old Damascus in May 2001. The 81-year-old pontiff took off his shoes and shuffled across the floor of the mosque, arm-in-arm with Syria's 86-year-old grand mufti, Sheikh Ahmad Kuftaro. The image of these two aging spiritual leaders in fraternal embrace had wide international resonance, especially in the Arab world. It soon attracted a sizable number of Muslim participants at the open-air Mass celebrated by the pope in the capital city of Astana, Kazakhstan, just two weeks after the September 11 tragedy in the United States.

John Paul II's encyclical on the Church's commitment to ecumenism, *Ut Unum Sint,* was released on May 25, 1995. In this remarkably candid and passionate appeal for Christian unity, John Paul II left no doubt about his own commitment and that of the Roman Catholic Church to the cause of ecumenism. Not only did this encyclical review many of the basic principles of true ecumenism and outline some of the major issues to be dealt with, but the pope even went so far as to invite Catholic and other religious leaders to undertake with him "a patient and fraternal dialogue" on the subject of the primacy of the bishop of Rome, which is "open to a new situation."[2]

In the spirit of promoting peace and collaboration among followers of various world religions, John Paul II called for a multireligious assembly to pray and fast for world peace in Assisi, home of St. Francis, on four occasions (in 1986, 1993, 1999, and 2001). The Holy Father's invitation was graciously accepted by hundreds of representatives of more than fifteen religious traditions—including Orthodox and Protestant Christians, Buddhists, Hindus, Muslims, Sikhs, Zoroastrians, and members of traditional African and Native American religions. Each religious group prayed in the manner and in the language of its respective tradition. Like every other participant, John Paul II came as a pilgrim who believed in prayer as the first step on the path to peace and unity.

At the Assisi celebration of October 27, 1986, the Holy Father explained the meaning of the celebration by underlining the fundamental unity of the human race in its origin and its destiny and the role of the Church as an effective sign of this unity. He emphasized the significance of interreligious dialogue, while at the same time reaffirming the Church's duty to proclaim and witness to the world that Jesus Christ is Lord and Savior of all.

Pause: What makes John Paul II's legacy in the areas of ecumenical and interreligious dialogue important in today's world?

JOHN PAUL II'S WORDS

We proceed along the road leading to the conversion of hearts guided by love which is directed to God and, at the same time, to all our brothers and sisters, including those not in full communion with us. Love gives rise to the desire for unity, even in those who have never been aware of the need for it. Love builds communion between individuals and between Communities. If we love one another, we strive to deepen our communion and make it perfect. Love is given to God as the perfect source of communion—the unity of Father, Son, and Holy Spirit—that we may draw from that source the strength to build communion between individuals and communities, or to re-establish it between Christians still divided. Love is the great undercurrent which gives life and adds vigor to the movement towards unity.

This love finds its most complete expression in common prayer. When brothers and sisters who are not in perfect communion with one another come together to pray . . . this prayer is "a very effective means of petitioning for the grace of unity," "a genuine expression of the ties which even now bind Catholics to their separated brethren." Even when prayer is not specifically offered for Christian unity, but for other intentions such as peace, it actually becomes an expression and confirmation of unity. The common prayer of Christians is an invitation to Christ himself to visit the community of those who call upon him: "Where two or three are gathered in my name, there am I in the midst of them" (Matthew 18:20).[3]

REFLECTION

"That they may all be one" (John 17:21). In making Jesus' prayer for unity our own, it helps to remember that he prayed this prayer when the hour had come for his passion and death. The unity that he prayed for was not unity in the interest of mere civility, but a unity of true communion "in which he wishes to embrace all people." It is not something added on, but stands at the very heart of Christ's mission.[4] As Christ's disciples, we are called to exhibit Christ's love for all people—to allow it to be made manifest through us and to permeate every encounter with fellow Christians as well as with followers of other religions.

When we look deeply into the things that divide us from fellow Christians and non-Christians alike, we can often detect preconceived ideas, festering wounds from the past, pride, prejudice—in short, the sin of division. It takes nothing less than dying to ourselves to completely overcome our tendency to sin in this way. John Paul II teaches us that if we are to truly follow Christ on his path of unity, we must start with prayer, repentance, reconciliation, and the renewal of our own Church. It is in a change of heart and in holiness of life, along with public and private prayer, that the Holy Spirit can surprise us with a restoration of unity among God's people that surpasses all expectation.

Questions for personal reflection and faith sharing:

❧ Have I played a role in causing or maintaining divisions between the Catholic Church and followers of other spiritual traditions? How can I live out Christ's prayer to overcome these divisions while faithfully upholding the fullness of truth in Christ and in the Church?

❧ What is at the heart of the challenges that I've encountered in relating to people of other religious traditions?

❧ What events and experiences in my past helped form my present attitudes toward other Christian or non-Christian traditions? How have these attitudes, positive or negative, affected my relationships with followers of these traditions? How might God be calling me to change the ways that I relate to people of other faiths in order to better serve Christ's call for unity?

Guidance for prayer and action:

❧ Reflect upon relationships in your life that have been marred or compromised by conflicts in religious belief. Recall the occasions when these conflicts became manifest, and how you dealt with them. Ask yourself the following questions: "Did I have it in my heart to say or do something that caused or contributed to the conflict? Have I failed to share my faith in love and in charity? Have I responded with love and forgiveness when confronted with an uncharitable deed or word? Did I simply ignore the conflict without making an effort toward dialogue?" Confess whatever sin of division you may committed, and pray for the grace to see Christ in every one of these people. Ask the Holy Spirit to grant you and all those concerned the grace of reconciliation and an openness to meaningful dialogue. End your reflection with the Lord's Prayer.

❧ Participate in the Week of Prayer for Christian Unity, traditionally observed from January 18 to 25 each year. John Paul II taught, "If Christians, despite their divisions, can grow more united in common prayer around Christ, they will grow in awareness of how little divides them in comparison with what unites them."[5]

❧ Before engaging in any ecumenical or interreligious encounter, pray Jesus' prayer "that they may all be one; even as thou, Father, art in me, and I in thee" (John 17:21), and ask the Holy Spirit to bless your encounter with his presence. You may also ask for the aid of the great saints of interfaith dialogue, such as St. Peter, St. Paul, St. Francis of Assisi, and Sts. Cyril and Methodius, to help you to be a faithful witness to Jesus Christ in these encounters.

❧ Extend hospitality to all persons who don't share your faith, especially those in religiously diverse marriages. Invite them to come to church events and family gatherings. Pray that these gatherings will help build unity among all those present.

❧ Consider participating in ecumenical activities that your parish or diocese sponsors. For example, some parishes offer annual interfaith services with neighboring churches. The *Directory for the Application of Principles and Norms on Ecumenism*, issued by the Pontifical Council for Promoting Christian Unity in 1993, vastly expands previous directives for participating in the ecumenical movement for all segments of the Church. This document, along with the Vatican II document *Nostra Aetate* and documents from the Pontifical Council for Interreligious Dialogue, are available at the Vatican Web site: www.vatican.va.

GOD'S WORD

Sanctify them in the truth; thy word is truth. As thou didst send me into the world, so I have sent them into the world. And for their sake I consecrate myself, that they also may be consecrated in truth.

I do not pray for these only, but also for those who believe in me through their word, that they may all be one; even as thou, Father, art in me, and I in thee, that they also may be in us, so that the world may believe that thou hast sent me.

—John 17:17-21

Closing prayer: Lord Jesus, grant us the grace of a heart ever united with you, the Father, and the Holy Spirit, in prayer and in deed. Let this communion with you be the center of our work for unity within the Church and with our encounters with all people. Amen.

1. John Paul II, *Crossing the Threshold of Hope,* p. 96.
2. John Paul II, Encyclical Letter *Ut Unum Sint* (On Commitment to Ecumenism), May 25, 1995, 95.
3. John Paul II, *Ut Unum Sint,* 21.
4. John Paul II, *Ut Unum Sint,* 9.
5. John Paul II, *Ut Unum Sint,* 22.

Truth and Freedom

Theme: Living according to God's truth is the only way to experience authentic freedom.

Opening prayer: Father, I thank you for the freedom to know and to love you. Help me to anchor my life in your Son, who is Truth, so that I can live a life of perfect freedom in total obedience to your will.

ABOUT JOHN PAUL II

What is freedom if it is not lived in truth? This is a question that occupied the mind of Karol Wojtyla for much of his life as he sought to understand the senseless destruction of two world wars and the dehumanizing effects of repressive ideologies and errant philosophies that swept through western civilization during the twentieth century.

Having studied philosophy extensively as a seminarian and throughout the years of his priesthood, John Paul II was well versed in the thinking of the age. He knew that the human person, although hindered by the wound of sin, was created for and is capable of true freedom. To this extent, he appreciated modernity's emphasis on freedom. Yet he also saw that modern secular philosophies that valued personal freedom over truth, and that promoted conscience as the arbiter of moral law rather than its vehicle, were intellectually dissatisfying and morally disastrous. When freedom was disassociated from truth, it became an excuse for license—an abuse of freedom that, rather than leading to a more fulfilling life, was ultimately dehumanizing and destructive. John Paul II was also aware that the confusion of modern men and women about who they are, where they come from, and where they are going often led to doubt, depression, and self-destruction.

Throughout his papacy, John Paul II fought tirelessly for basic human freedoms, but never at the expense of truth, even when the Church's stance on various moral issues was unpopular. In 1993, after years of reflection, he wrote *Veritatis Splendor* (The Splendor of Truth), the first extensive analysis by a pope of the foundations of human morality and the role of truth in moral life. In it he addressed the destructive results of divorcing freedom from truth and the resulting confusion between good and evil that had reached crisis proportions in the world. This confusion was experienced in the individual conscience, in family and community life, in the academic world, and in courts of law. He not only clarified fundamental misunderstandings but called for a reorienting of life toward truth and emphasized the importance of relating freedom to truth. As he put it repeatedly, "Authentic freedom is ordered to truth."[1]

Pause: How do I understand freedom in relation to truth?

JOHN PAUL II'S WORDS

Christ reveals, first and foremost, that the frank and open acceptance of truth is the condition for authentic freedom: "You will know the truth, and the truth will set you free" (John 8:32). This is truth which sets one free in the face of worldly power. . . . So it was with Jesus before Pilate: "For this I was born, and for this I have come into the world, to bear witness to the truth" (John 18:37).[2]

The true worshippers of God must thus worship him "in spirit and truth" (John 4:23): in this worship they become free. Worship of God and a relationship with truth are revealed in Jesus Christ as the deepest foundation of freedom. Furthermore, Jesus reveals by his whole life, and not only by his words, that freedom is acquired in love, that is, in the gift of self. The one who says: "Greater love has no man than this, that a man lay down his life for his friends" (John 15:13) freely goes out to meet his Passion (Matthew 26:46), and in obedience to the Father gives his life on the Cross for all men (Philippians 2:6-11).[3]

Contemplation of Jesus Crucified is thus the highroad which the Church must tread every day if she wishes to understand the full meaning of freedom: the gift of self in service to God and one's brethren. Communion with the Crucified and Risen Lord is the never-ending source from which the Church draws unceasingly in order to live in freedom, to give of herself and to serve. . . . Jesus, then, is the living, personal summation of perfect freedom in total obedience to the will of God. His crucified flesh fully reveals the unbreakable bond between freedom and truth, just as his Resurrection from the dead is the supreme exaltation of the fruitfulness and saving power of a freedom lived out in truth.[4]

Reflection

An instance of the moral confusion that John Paul II refers to in *Veritatis Splendor* was described by a Jesuit priest. A class was invited to consider a typical moral dilemma that might be faced by a young woman. This was the dialogue that ensued: Teacher: "So those are the choices open to her. What should she do?" Students: "It's up to her." Teacher: "Yes, I know it's up to her. But what should she do?" Students: "It's her choice." Teacher: "Yes, we know it's her choice. But how should she choose? And on what grounds?" Students: "It's her choice."[5]

Who of us have not witnessed the painful reality that underlies such an exchange—the abandonment of any sense of personal commitment to moral truth that has become so prevalent in our world? Severed relationships, a sense of brokenness, and confusion about one's identity and the source and meaning of life have resulted from a use of freedom separated from truth. How many in our world suffer the desolation of the deepest sense of alienation—the loss of communion with God, all for the sake of personal freedom and autonomy!

In *Veritatis Splendor,* John Paul II asks us to pray that all people will seek to reestablish their lives on the deepest foundation of truth and freedom—to anchor their lives in Jesus Christ, who is the way, the truth, and the life.

Questions for personal reflection and faith sharing:

❧ How have I experienced the crisis of truth that John Paul II speaks of? How has this experience helped me to know and to follow Jesus Christ as the way, the truth, and the life?

❧ How do I experience true freedom as a result of worshipping God in spirit and in truth (John 4:23)?

❧ How has my understanding of freedom changed through the years? What has helped me the most in deepening my understanding of what true freedom entails?

❧ What currents of thought have I encountered in my education or in the world that have pulled me away from a commitment to Christian teaching on truth and freedom? What impact have these philosophies had on my life?

Guidance for prayer and action:

❧ In prayer, ask for help in purifying and forming your conscience to become "the witness of God himself, whose voice and judgment penetrate the depths of man's soul."[6] Ask yourself,

"Am I living in perfect freedom, that is, in total obedience to the will of God? What weaknesses bind me from living the full meaning of freedom—the gift of self in service to God and my brothers and sisters? Am I willing to lay down my life for all those I am called to serve? Have I been a loving witness to Jesus, who is the Truth?" As a means of purifying your conscience and anchoring it in truth, celebrate the Sacraments of Reconciliation and the Eucharist frequently.

ϟ When faced with a moral dilemma, prayerfully read the portion of the *Catechism of the Catholic Church* that addresses your specific problem. Pray to the Holy Spirit to lead you into all truth about the situation (see John 14:16-17). Let Christ's words sink deeply into your heart and guide your conscience: "If you love me, you will keep my commandments" (John 14:15); "You will know the truth, and the truth will set you free" (John 8:32).

ϟ Reflect upon a time in your life when you experienced an internal battle between doing what you wanted or doing God's will. Describe what it was like to go through this, and how you went about making the decision that you made. If your conscience failed to point you in the direction of truth, reflect upon how this happened. (Was it due to a lack of conscience formation? A lack of prayer and faithfulness to God's law?) What was the outcome of your choice? What lessons have you learned from this experience? How has this experience helped you to know Christ as the Truth that sets one free? End your reflection by praising and thanking God for his steadfast love and faithfulness. Consider passing this on as part of your spiritual legacy to loved ones.

❧ What can you and your family do to stand up for truth in the world? Perhaps you can become involved in the pro-life movement or in the fight against pornography. Remember, every voice can make a difference. Pray, "Lord, what would you have me do today to more fully live the truth, and to help the world see the splendor of truth?"

GOD'S WORD

For this I was born, and for this I have come into the world, to bear witness to the truth. Every one who is of the truth hears my voice.

—John 18:37

Closing prayer: O Mary, Mother of Mercy, watch over us so that we may not stray from the path of the good or become blind to sin. May all people put their hope in God, who is rich in mercy (Ephesians 2:4). May we carry out the good works prepared by God beforehand so that we can live completely for the praise of his glory (Ephesians 2:10; 1:12).[7] Amen.

1. John Paul II, Encyclical Letter *Veritatis Splendor* (Splendor of Truth), August 6, 1993, 87.

2. John Paul II, *Veritatis Splendor*, 87.

3. John Paul II, *Veritatis Splendor*, 87.

4. John Paul II, *Veritatis Splendor*, 87.

5. John Wilkins, ed. *Considering Veritatis Splendor* (Cleveland: Pilgrim Press, 1994), p. 10.

6. John Paul II, *Veritatis Splendor*, 58.

7. Adapted from John Paul II, *Veritatis Splendor*, 120.

MEDITATION FIFTEEN

The Springtime of Evangelization

Theme: Witnessing to the faith is a Christian's fundamental calling.

Opening prayer: We thank you, Father, for making yourself and your love known to us through your Son, and for all the witnesses you have sent our way. We thank you for the faithfulness of your servant, Pope John Paul II, who has prepared the Church for a new springtime of evangelization. Lord, let your Spirit clothe your bride, the Church, with power and the grace to labor in joy to bear infinite fruit in your kingdom.

ABOUT JOHN PAUL II

On numerous occasions, John Paul II proclaimed the dawning of a "new springtime," "a new missionary age," in which Christians will need to spread the gospel primarily by pursuing the path of holiness, and by employing fresh methods to communicate Christ's saving power to as many people as possible. There could be no better example of this new evangelization than the witness of John Paul II himself, who not only lived a holy life, but made use of every possible means to deliver the message that "in God alone can the human heart find peace and complete happiness."[1]

More than any pope before him, John Paul II personally connected with the people he served. He literally took the papacy on the road, visiting 129 countries and covering a staggering 723,000 miles—more than all other popes combined. Called the "media pope" for his skillful use of television, radio, and the Internet, John Paul II delivered more than two thousand speeches and hundreds of homilies, and published best-selling books. He spoke the language of the world's youth, identified with people who were suffering or oppressed, and demonstrated to the elderly what it truly means to live and to die with dignity. In all of these encounters, John Paul II gave uncompromising testimony to the gospel and inspired countless people to become evangelizers themselves.

Whenever people referred to him as one of the greatest evangelizers of all time, John Paul II was always quick to point to the Holy Spirit as "the principal evangelizer."[2] One such occasion, when the Holy Spirit set a multitude of hearts on fire for the Lord, was Pentecost '98, a world congress of ecclesial movements and new communities, where the pope met with half a million members of at least fifty worldwide lay movements. A journalist whose family happened to be in Rome at the time reported her experience of the event: "Never in my twenty-some-year career as a journalist have I witnessed anything like this. It felt like the rebirth of the Church. All day, all over Rome, from all directions, the multitudes just swarmed toward St. Peter's Square in great masses, usually singing and waving flags. . . . The very sight and sound and energy of it was glorious. At one point, I thought of the transfiguration, and like St. Peter, I wanted to just pitch a tent and stay there forever. It was a new birth for the Church, a new sending forth of apostles on fire to spread the 'good news.'"[3]

To prepare them for their mission in the Church, John Paul II told those gathered at Pentecost '98, "The Church expects from you the 'mature fruits' of communion and commitment. . . . You have learned . . . that faith is not abstract talk, nor vague religious sentiment, but new life in Christ instilled by the Holy Spirit. . . . Today, from this square, Christ says to each of you: 'Go into all the world and preach the gospel to the whole creation' (Mark 16:15). He is counting on every one of you, and so is the Church. 'Lo,' the Lord promises, 'I am with you always to the close of the age' (Matthew 28:20). I am with you. Amen!"[4]

Pause: How is the Lord calling me to participate in the Church's springtime of evangelization?

JOHN PAUL II'S WORDS

Today, as never before, the Church has the opportunity of bringing the Gospel, by witness and word, to all people and nations. I see the dawning of a new missionary age, which will become a radiant day bearing an abundant harvest, if all Christians . . . respond with generosity and holiness to the calls and challenges of our time.[5]

There is room for everyone in the Lord's vineyard. No one is so poor that he has nothing to give; no one so rich that he has nothing to receive.[6]

The world today needs to see your love for Christ. . . . As Paul VI once said: "Modern man listens more willingly to witnesses than to teachers, and if he listens to teachers he does so because they are witnesses." If the nonbelievers of this world are to believe in Christ, they need your faithful testimony—testimony that springs from your complete trust in the generous mercy of the Father and in your enduring faith in the power of the cross and of the resurrection. Thus the ideals, the values, the convictions that are the basis of your dedication to Christ must be translated into the language of daily life. . . . Your public testimony is part of your contribution to the mission of the Church. As St. Paul says: "You are a letter from Christ . . . written not with ink but with the Spirit of the living God, not on tablets of stone but on tablets of human hearts."[7]

REFLECTION

Although many of us have never considered ourselves to be evangelizers, John Paul II reminds us that we *are* evangelizers by virtue of our baptism in Jesus Christ. That Christ entrusted the great commission (Matthew 28:19-20) to all his disciples means that this commission is written on our hearts as a fundamental calling. In our homes, in our workplaces, in our communities—and in everything we do—we are called to witness by our actions and our words to God's love for the world. In God's eyes, our faithful witness is just as important a response to God's call to evangelize as the witness of even the pope himself.

The new evangelization John Paul II speaks of is, in essence, not so much about trying to convert greater numbers of people to Christianity, but about what the Holy Spirit can do through us when we are open and docile to his inspiration and direction. The Church has grown from a handful of disciples on the first Pentecost to over a billion strong, not by the works of men and women, but by the work of the Holy Spirit in those who have generously shared with others what God has done for them.

For us, as for the earliest Christians, the challenges of witnessing to the faith are many and oftentimes complex. These challenges may be internal, such as a lack of confidence, or external, such as hostility toward Christian witness. But God conquers these challenges for us when we offer them to him in prayer and allow him to transform our weaknesses into the love that it takes to share our faith in charity and in truth.

Questions for personal reflection and faith sharing:

  What have I learned from John Paul II's work as an evangelizer? What can I take from his example to apply in my own life as a Christian witness?

  What challenges have I faced in the past when I was given the opportunity to witness to my faith? How did I respond to these challenges, and how did these experiences help to strengthen my faith?

❧ How have I experienced the Holy Spirit's work in bringing about a new springtime of evangelization in the Church (e.g., in my own life, within my parish, in my diocese, or in some Church movement with which I'm familiar)? What has this experience taught me about what it means to evangelize in love and in charity?

Guidance for prayer and action:

❧ Reflect upon how God has been preparing a springtime in your life as a Christian witness. Think of occasions when you felt compelled to stand up for what you believe, and how your faith was strengthened by your willingness to profess it. Ask forgiveness for the times when you failed to respond to God's call in full measure. Offer to God all the difficulties and frustrations you have experienced in witnessing to your faith. Ask the Holy Spirit to dwell in you and work through you in every situation in which God calls you to witness in his name.

❧ Pray any one or all of these verses repeatedly, letting Christ's words resound in your heart: "Follow me, and I will make you fishers of men" (Matthew 4:19); "Go therefore and make disciples of all nations" (Matthew 28:19); "I came to cast fire upon the earth; and would that it were already kindled!" (Luke 12:49).

❧ Read John Paul II's major writings on the new evangelization and reflect upon how God may be calling you to evangelize according to your vocation in life and your particular gifts. These documents include the post-synodal apostolic exhortations *Christifideles Laici* (On the Vocation and the Mission of the Lay Faithful in the Church and in the World), *Pastores Dabo Vobis* (On the Formation of Priests in the Circumstances of the Present Day), *Vita Consecrata* (On the Consecrated Life and Its Mission in the Church and in the World), and *Ecclesia in America* (The Church in America). They can be found at the Vatican Web site.

❧ Take account of the talents God has given you. Thank God for each one of them. Then ask how he would want you to use these gifts to share your faith with others. Write down any number of ways that come to mind, and ask the Holy Spirit to guide you in the steps you need to take to put these gifts to use. Perhaps you could join a group or help form a group in your parish or diocese engaged in evangelization.

❧ Pray for an increase in vocations. Couple your prayers with efforts among family and friends to consider entering the religious life, or inspire them to be witnesses to the faith, whatever their vocation may be.

❧ Do you financially support missions in the Church or other groups that evangelize? If so, pray about whether you can increase your giving. If not, ask your pastor to suggest organizations you could support that do the work of evangelization in the Church.

GOD'S WORD

And Jesus came and said to them, "All authority in heaven and on earth has been given to me. Go therefore and make disciples of all nations, baptizing them in the name of the Father and of the Son and of the Holy Spirit, teaching them to observe all that I have commanded you; and lo, I am with you always, to the close of the age."

—Matthew 28:18-20

Closing prayer: "Come, Holy Spirit, come and renew the face of the earth! Come with your seven gifts! Come, Spirit of Life, Spirit of Communion and Love! The Church and the world need you. Come, Holy Spirit, and make ever more fruitful the charisms you have bestowed on us. Give new strength and missionary zeal to these sons and daughters of yours who have gathered here. Open their hearts; renew their Christian commitment to the world. Make them courageous messengers of the Gospel, witnesses to the risen Jesus Christ, the Redeemer and Savior of man. Strengthen their love and their fidelity to the Church."[8] Amen.

1. John Paul II, Encounter with Representatives of "All the Generations of This Century," Aztec Stadium, Mexico City, January 25, 1999, 12.
2. John Paul II, Synod of Bishops, Special Assembly for America: Encounter with the Living Jesus Christ: The Way to

Conversion, Communion and Solidarity in America, Vatican City, 1996, 14.

3. Sheila Gribben Liaugminas, "A Renewed Pentecost: Catholic Movements Called to a New Dynamism," *Voices*, December 1998.

4. John Paul II, Meeting with Ecclesial Movements and New Communities, 6–7, 9.

5. John Paul II, Encyclical Letter *Redemptoris Missio* (On the Permanent Validity of the Church's Missionary Mandate), December 7, 1990, 92.

6. John Paul II, Address to the Bishops Taking Part in the Course of Formation Organized by the Congregation for the Evangelization of Peoples, September 19, 2003, 3.

7. John Paul II, Homily, February 17, 1981, Philippines, 3.

8. John Paul II, Meeting with Ecclesial Movements and New Communities, 9.

Works Cited

Barnes, Jane, and Helen Whitney. "John Paul II and the Fall of Communism." *Frontline*, PBS, September 28, 1999. www.pbs.org/wgbh/pages/frontline/shows/pope/communism/.

Bernstein, Carl, and Marco Politi. *His Holiness.* New York: Doubleday, 1996.

"Biography of John Paul II." www.vatican.va/holy_father/john_paul_ii/.

Boczula, Dominika. "I Took the Pope's Word to Heart," *Western Catholic Reporter,* September 9, 2002. www.wcr.ab.ca/index.shtml.

The Catholic Encyclopedia, online edition, s.v. "Didache," (by John Chapman), www.newadvent.org/cathen/04779a.htm (accessed March 28, 2006).

Gray, Paul. "Man of the Year: Empire of the Spirit." *Time,* December 26, 1994.

"History of World Youth Day." www.wyd.ie/history.html.

The Catholic Encyclopedia, online edition, s.v. "St. Ignatius of

Antioch," (by John B. O'Connor), www.newadvent.org/cathen/07644a.htm (accessed March 15, 2006).

The Catholic Encyclopedia, online edition, s.v. *"Adversus Haereses,"* Ireneaus, *Contra Haereticos* (edited by Alexander Roberts & James Donaldson), www.newadvent.org/fathers/0103418.htm (accessed March 21, 2006).

John Paul II. Address to the Bishops Taking Part in the Course of Formation Organized by the Congregation for the Evangelization of Peoples. September 19, 2003. www.vatican.va/holy_father/john_paul_ii/speeches/2003/september/documents/hf_jp-ii_spe_20030919_bishops-mission_en.html.

John Paul II. Address to the Secular Institute "Servants of Suffering." December 2, 2004. www.vatican.va/holy_father/john_paul_ii/speeches/2004/december/documents/hf_jp-ii_spe_20041202_servi-sofferenza_en.html.

John Paul II. Address to Seminarians, Pontifical Major Seminary of Rome. October 22, 1987. The Teachings of John Paul II on CD-ROM. Salem, OR: Harmony Media, Inc., 1998.

John Paul II. Address to the United Nations General Assembly. October 5, 1995. www.vatican.va/holy_father/john_paul_ii/speeches/1995/october/documents/hf_jp-ii_spe_05101995_address-to-uno_en.html.

John Paul II. Address at Vespers at Saint Joseph's Seminary, New York. October 6, 1995. www.ewtn.com/library/ PAPALDOC/JP2US95G.HTM.

John Paul II. Address at the World Meeting of Families. October 8, 1994. www.bethanyfamilyinstitute.com/ AddressWMF1994.htm.

John Paul II. Apostolic Exhortations *Christifideles Laici* (December 30, 1988), *Ecclesia in America* (January 22, 1999), *Familiaris Consortio* (November 22, 1981), *Pastores Dabo Vobis* (March 25, 1992), *Reconciliatio et Paenitentia* (December 2, 1984), and *Vita Consecrata* (March 25, 1996). www.vatican.va/holy_father/john_paul_ii/apost_ exhortations/.

John Paul II. Apostolic Letter *Master in the Faith*. December 14, 1990. www.ewtn.com/library/PAPALDOC/JPMASTER. HTM.

John Paul II. Apostolic Letters *Mulieris Dignitatem* (August 15, 1988), *Novo Millennio Ineunte* (January 6, 2001), *Rosarium Virginis Mariae* (October 16, 2002), and *Salvifici Doloris* (February 11, 1984). www.vatican.va/holy_father/ john_paul_ii/apost_letters/index.htm.

John Paul II. *Crossing the Threshold of Hope*. Edited by Vittorio Messori. New York: Alfred A. Knopf, 1994.

John Paul II. Encounter with Representatives of "All the Generations of This Century." Aztec Stadium, Mexico City. January 25, 1999. www.ewtn.com/jp99/words25.htm.

John Paul II. Encyclical Letter *Dominum et Vivificantem* (May 18, 1986), *Ecclesia de Eucharistia* (April 4, 2003), *Evangelium Vitae* (March 25, 1995), *Redemptoris Mater* (March 25, 1987), *Redemptoris Missio* (December 7, 1990), *Ut Unum Sint* (May 25, 1995), and *Veritatis Splendor* (August 6, 1993). www.vatican.va/holy_father/john_paul_ii/encyclicals/index.htm.

John Paul II. General Audience. May 30, 1979. The Teachings of John Paul II on CD-ROM. Salem, OR: Harmony Media, Inc., 1998.

John Paul II. General Audience. June 8, 1983. The Teachings of John Paul II on CD-ROM. Salem, OR: Harmony Media, Inc., 1998.

John Paul II. General Audience. July 10, 2002. www.vatican.va/holy_father/john_paul_ii/audiences/2002/documents/hf_jp-ii_aud_20020710_en.html.

John Paul II. *Gift and Mystery*. New York: Doubleday, 1996.

John Paul II. Homily. February 17, 1981. Philippines. The Teachings of John Paul II on CD-ROM. Salem, OR:

Harmony Media, Inc., 1998.

John Paul II. Homily. Celebration for John Paul II's 50th Jubilee of Priestly Ordination. November 7, 1996. The Teachings of John Paul II on CD-ROM. Salem, OR: Harmony Media, Inc., 1998.

John Paul II. Homily. Divine Mercy Sunday. April 22, 2001. www.vatican.va/holy_father/john_paul_ii/homilies/2001/index.htm.

John Paul II. Homily. Eucharistic Celebration on the Occasion of the World Meeting with Families. October 9, 1994. The Teachings of John Paul II on CD-ROM. Salem, OR: Harmony Media, Inc., 1998.

John Paul II. Homily. First International Congress of the Focolare Movement, April 30, 1982. The Teachings of John Paul II on CD-ROM. Salem, OR: Harmony Media, Inc., 1998.

John Paul II. Homily. Mass in the Trans World Dome, St. Louis. January 27, 1999. www.vatican.va/holy_father/john_paul_ii/homilies/1999/index.htm.

John Paul II. Homily. Mass in Victory Square, Warsaw. June 2, 1979. The Teachings of John Paul II on CD-ROM. Salem, OR: Harmony Media, Inc., 1998.

John Paul II. Homily. Mass for the Canonization of Sister Mary Faustina Kowalska. April 30, 2000. www.vatican.va/holy_father/john_paul_ii/homilies/2000/index.htm.

John Paul II. Homily. Pontifical Athenaeum in Pune. February 10, 1986. www.vatican.va/holy_father/john_paul_ii/homilies/1986/index.htm.

John Paul II. Homily. Prato, Italy. March 19, 1986. The Teachings of John Paul II on CD-ROM. Salem, OR: Harmony Media, Inc., 1998.

John Paul II. Homily at Aqueduct Racetrack. October 6, 1995. www.ewtn.com/library/PAPALDOC/JP2US95F.htm.

John Paul II. Homily on Fidelity to the Priestly Vocation. Olaya Herrera Airport of Medellin. July 5, 1986. The Teachings of John Paul II on CD-ROM. Salem, OR: Harmony Media, Inc., 1998.

John Paul II. Homily on the Solemnity of the Assumption. August 15, 1997. www.vatican.va/holy_father/john_paul_ii/homilies/1997/index.htm.

John Paul II. *Incarnationis Mysterium.* Bull of Indiction of the Great Jubilee of the Year 2000. November 29, 1998. www.vatican.va/jubilee_2000/docs/index.htm.

John Paul II. *Letter to the Elderly.* October 1, 1999. www.vatican.va/holy_father/john_paul_ii/letters/documents/hf_jp-ii_let_01101999_elderly_en.html.

John Paul II. May 30, 1979. The Teachings of John Paul II on CD-ROM. Salem, OR: Harmony Media, Inc., 1998.

John Paul II. Meeting with Ecclesial Movements and New Communities. May 30, 1998. www.catholic-jhb.org.za/articles/movement98.htm.

John Paul II. Papal Discourse on the 5th Anniversary of *Evangelium Vitae.* February 14, 2000. www.catholic-forum.com/saintS/pope0264ja.htm.

John Paul II. Prayer for the Family, Themes for Reflection and Dialogue for the Fourth World Meeting of the Family. January 25–26, 2003. www.vatican.va/roman_curia/pontifical_councils/family/documents/rc_pc_family_doc_20020412_iv-meeting-families-manila_en.html.

John Paul II. *The Private Prayers of John Paul II.* trans. Ann Goldstein. New York: Pocket Books, 1994.

John Paul II. 17th World Youth Day Papal Welcoming Ceremony Address. Toronto. July 25, 2002. www.vatican.va/holy_father/john_paul_ii/speeches/2002/july/documents/hf_jp-ii_spe_20020725_wyd-address-youth_en.html.

John Paul II. *Springtime of the New Evangelization: The Complete Texts of the Holy Father's 1998 Ad. Limina Addresses to the Bishops of the United States.* Edited by Thomas D. Williams. San Francisco: Ignatius Press, 1999.

John Paul II. Synod of Bishops. Special Assembly for America: Encounter with the Living Jesus Christ: The Way to Conversion, Communion and Solidarity in America. Vatican City. 1996. www.vatican.va/roman_curia/synod/documents/rc_synod_doc_01081996_usa-lincam_en.html.

John Paul II. *Theology of the Body: Human Love in the Divine Plan.* Boston: Pauline Books and Media, 1997.

John Paul II with representatives of the Roman Curia. *Universal Prayer: Confessions of Sins and Asking for Forgiveness.* March 12, 2000.

"John Paul II's Last Words: Vatican Publishes the Final 'Stations' of His Way of the Cross." Zenit News Agency. Sept. 21, 2005. www.zenit.org/english/visualizza.phtml?sid=76861.

The Catholic Encyclopedia, online edition, s.v. "Justin Martyr, First Apology," www.newadvent.org/fathers/0126.htm.

Knights of Columbus Prayer for Married Couples. www.communitynews.org/kc_folder/Newsletters_01/February_2001.htm.

Kwitney, Jonathan. *Man of the Century: The Life and Times of John Paul II*. New York: Henry Holt & Company, Inc., 1997.

Liaugminas, Sheila Gribben. "A Renewed Pentecost: Catholic Movements Called to a New Dynamism," *Voices*, December 1998. www.wf-f.org/liaugminas98.html.

Vatican Council II. *Lumen Gentium* (Dogmatic Constitution on the Church), November 21, 1964. www.vatican.va/archive/hist_councils/ii_vatican_council/documents/vat-ii_const_19641121_lumen-gentium_en.html.

Weigel, George. *Witness to Hope*. New York: HarperCollins, 2001.

"What World Leaders Say about Pope John Paul II" Zenit News Agency. April 10, 2005. www.yourcatholicvoice.org/insight.php?article=2023.

Wilkins, John, ed. *Considering Veritatis Splendor.* Cleveland: The Pilgrim Press, 1994.

Additional Resources

Books by Karol Wojtyla

Wojtyla, Karol. *The Jeweler's Shop.* Translated by Boleslaw Taborski. San Francisco: Ignatius Press, 1992.

Wojtyla, Karol. *Love and Responsibility.* Translated by H. T. Willets. San Francisco: Ignatius Press, 1991.

Resources on John Paul II's Life and Work

Boniecki, Adam. *The Making of the Pope of the Millennium: Kalendarium of the Life of Karol Wojtyla.* Stockbridge, MA: Marian Press, 2000.

Dulles, Avery. *The Splendor of Faith: The Theological Vision of Pope John Paul II.* New York: Crossroad Publishing, 1999.

Frossard, André. *Portrait of John Paul II.* San Francisco: Ignatius Press, 1990.

Gneuhs, Geoffrey, ed. *The Legacy of Pope John Paul II: His Contribution to Catholic Thought.* New York: The Crossroad Publishing Company, 2000.

Lawler, Ronald D. *The Christian Personalism of John Paul II.* Chicago: Franciscan Herald Press, 1982.

Neuhaus, Richard John. "The Splendor of Truth: A Symposium." *First Things: The Journal of Religion, Culture, and Public Life* 40 (January 1994): 14–29.

Schu, Walter. *John Paul II: Personal Study Guide to His Thought and Mission.* Thornwood, NY: Legion of Christ College, 1999.

Books on Catholic Pilgrimages

Copp, Jay. *The Liguori Guide to Catholic USA.* Liguori, MO: Liguori Publications, 1999.

National Conference of Catholic Bushops. *Catholic Shrines and Places of Pilgrimage in the United States* (Jubilee Edition). Washington, DC: National Conference of Catholic Bishops, 1998.

Books on Married Saints

Fink, John. *Married Saints.* Staten Island, NY: Alba House, 1999.

Ford, Mary, and David Ford. *Marriage as a Path to Holiness: Lives of Married Saints.* South Canaan, PA: STS Press, 1999.

Holbock, Ferdinand, and Michael J Miller. *Married Saints and Blesseds Through the Centuries*. Ft. Collins. CO: Ignatius Press, 2002.

Resources on the Theology of the Body and Catholic Sexual Ethics

Kellmeyer, Steven. *Sex and the Sacred City: Meditations on the Theology of the Body*. Peoria, IL: Bridegroom Press, 2003.

Lawler, Ronald, Joseph Boyle, and William May. *Catholic Sexual Ethics: A Summary, Explanation and Defense*. Second Edition. Huntington, IN: Our Sunday Visitor, 1999.

West, Christopher. *The Theology of the Body Explained, A Commentary on John Paul II's Gospel of the Body*. Boston: Pauline Books and Media, 2003.

Resources on Ecumenical and Interreligious Dialogue

Pontifical Council for Promoting Christian Unity. *Directory for the Application of Principles and Norms on Ecumenism*. www.vatican.va/roman_curia/pontifical_councils/chrstuni/ documents/rc_pc_chrstuni_doc_25031993_principles-and-norms-on-ecumenism_en.html.

Vatican Council II. *Nostra Aetate*. www.vatican.va/archive/ hist_councils/ii_vatican_council/documents/vat-ii_decl_

19651028_nostra-aetate_en.html.

Books on Lay Movements and the New Evangelization

Whitehead, Kenneth D., ed. *Voices of the New Springtime. The Life and Work of the Catholic Church in the 21st Century.* South Bend, IN: St. Augustine's Press, 2004.

United States Conference of Catholic Bishops. *Directory of Lay Movements, Organizations, and Professional Associations.* Washington, DC: USCCB, 2005.

Catholic Media Resources

Vatican Radio
"The Voice of the Pope and the Church in the World"
www.radiovaticana.org/inglese/enindex.html
Radio Vaticana Palazzo Pio Piazza
Pia 3 00120 Citta del Vaticano

Vatican newspaper *L'Osservatore Romano*
Weekly edition available online at www.vatican.va/news_
services/or/or_eng/
For English subscriptions, contact:
The Cathedral Foundation
PO Box 777
Baltimore, MD 21203
Phone: 410-547-5380

Eternal Word Television Network: Global Catholic Network
5817 Old Leeds Road
Irondale, AL 35210
www.ewtn.com

For a directory of Catholic newspapers, magazines, and book publishers, contact:
Catholic Press Association
3555 Veterans Memorial Highway, Unit O
Ronkonkoma, NY 11779
www.catholicpress.org

For a directory of Catholic radio stations, contact:
Catholic Radio Association
121 Broad Street
Charleston, SC 29401
www.catholicradioassociation.org

Zenit, an international news agency, provides objective coverage of events, documents, and issues emanating from or concerning the Catholic Church. To receive a free online subscription, go to www.zenit.org.

Catholic News Service
3211 Fourth St., NE
Washington, DC 20017
www.catholicnews.com

Also in the Companions for the Journey Series

Praying with Ignatius of Loyola
**Jacqueline Syrup Bergan and
Marie Schwan, CSJ**
Even after five centuries, Ignatius' spiritual exercises continue to lead men and women to commit their lives to Jesus. Wherever we are in our walk with the Lord, he challenges us to do all things for the glory of God.
160 pages, 5¼ x 8, softcover, $11.95
Item# BSMDE3

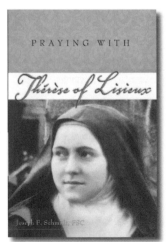

Praying with Thérèse of Lisieux
Joseph F. Schmidt, FSC
Thérèse knew that God led her, with all her inadequacies, to holiness. She assures us that God can do the same for us.
160 pages, 5¼ x 8, softcover, $11.95
Item# BSMUE3

To order call 1-800-775-9673 or order online at www.wordamongus.org